SMP **11-16**

Book B3

*The right of the
University of Cambridge
to print and sell
all manner of books
was granted by
Henry VIII in 1534.
The University has printed
and published continuously
since 1584.*

Cambridge University Press

Cambridge
London   New York   New Rochelle
Melbourne   Sydney

Published by the Press Syndicate of the University of Cambridge
The Pitt Building, Trumpington Street, Cambridge CB2 1RP
32 East 57th Street, New York, NY 10022, USA
10 Stamford Road, Oakleigh, Melbourne 3166, Australia

© Cambridge University Press 1986

First published 1986
Reprinted 1986

Illustrations by David Parkins
Diagrams and phototypesetting by Parkway Group, London and
Abingdon, and Gecko Limited, Bicester, Oxon.
Photographs by John Ling
Colour photography by Graham Portlock.

Printed in Great Britain at the University Press, Cambridge

British Library cataloguing in publication data
SMP 11–16 blue series.
  Bk B3
  1. Mathematics – 1961–
  I. School Mathematics Project
  510   QA39.2
  ISBN 0 521 31470 4

Contents

1 Cuboids

A Nets of a cube and a cuboid

This is a drawing of a cube.
In the drawing you can see 9 of its edges, and 7 of its corners (or **vertices**).

There are 3 more edges and one more **vertex** round the back of the cube.
The hidden edges can be shown by dotted lines, like this.

A cube has 6 square **faces**.
Imagine the cube to be made of card. The 6 faces can be 'opened out' by cutting along edges, like this.

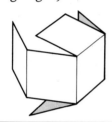

When the card is flattened out, it looks like this.

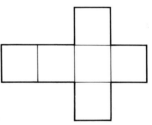

This is called a **net** of the cube.

This is also a net of a cube.

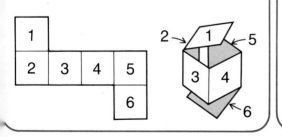

But this is **not** a net of a cube.

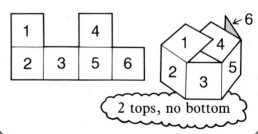

2 tops, no bottom

A1 Is this a net of a cube?
Draw it and cut it out if you are not sure.

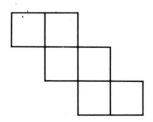

A2 Which of these are nets of a cube?
Try to answer without drawing and cutting out.

A
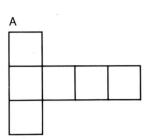

B
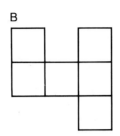

C
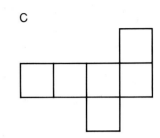

If you make a cube from paper or card, you need 'tabs' or 'flaps' to glue the paper or card together.

When we say 'net' we do not include tabs. These are something extra added to the net.

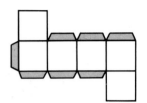

Every face of a cube is a square.
If every face of a solid is a **rectangle**, the solid is called a **cuboid**.

(A square is a special kind of rectangle, so a cube is a special kind of cuboid.)

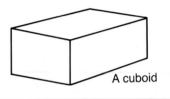

A cuboid

This cuboid is 2 cm by 3 cm by 4 cm . . .   . . . and here is a net for it.

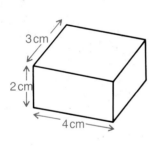

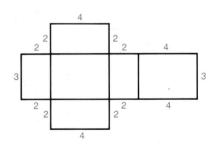

A3 Draw a net for this cuboid on squared paper.

Cut out the net and fold it to check that it is correct.

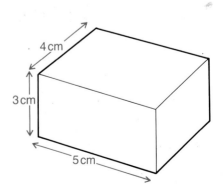

2

Cardboard boxes are often in the shape of a cuboid.
They are made flat and then folded.

This is an 'Oxo' box flattened out, full-size.
The glue for sticking it together goes in one place only, the
white rectangle on the flap at the bottom.

A4 Measure the flattened box to
find the length, width and
height of the box, to the
nearest centimetre.

3

Make your own box.

Draw this cut-out full-size on squared or spotty paper.
If you want to draw designs on the faces of your box,
do it before you cut and fold.

Cut out, and score and fold along the dotted lines. Stick your
box together.

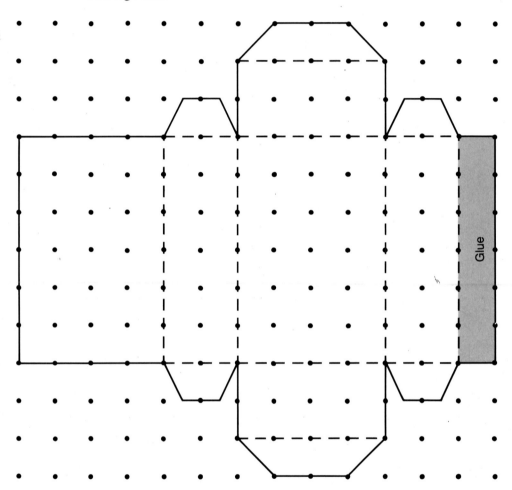

A6 Are these nets of cuboids? Try to answer without making them.

(a)

(b)

A7 Which of the drawings below are nets of cuboids?
Answer first without drawing or making them. Then check
any you are ensure about by making them.

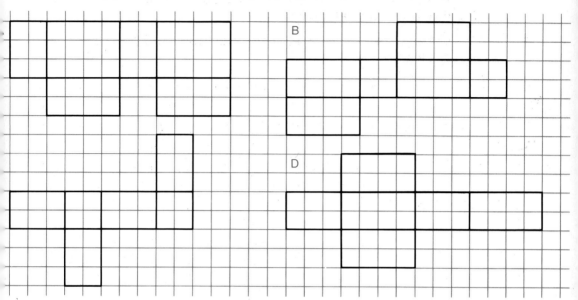

How to sketch a cuboid

First method

Start by drawing a rectangle.	Then draw another of the same size, like this.	Then join up like this.
	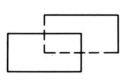	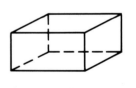

Second method

Start by drawing three lines like this.	Every other edge is **parallel** to one of those you drew at first.	You can show the hidden edges by dotted lines.
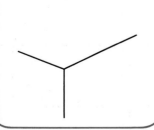	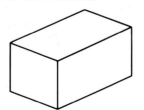	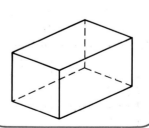

A8 Draw a sketch of a cuboid (a) by the first method (b) by the second

B The volume of a cuboid

Small volumes can be measured in **cubic centimetres** (cm³).
1 cm³ is the volume of a cube 1 cm by 1 cm by 1 cm.

This diagram shows that a cuboid 2 cm by 3 cm by 4 cm
can be split up into cubes, each of volume 1 cm³.

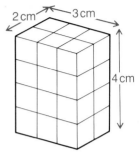

The cuboid consists of 4 layers.
Each layer contains $2 \times 3 = 6$ cubes.
So the total number of cubes is $6 \times 4 = \mathbf{24}$.

The simplest way to work out the volume is to
multiply the three measurements together.
$$2 \times 3 \times 4 = \mathbf{24\,cm^3}$$

B1 Calculate the volumes of the cuboids whose measurements
are given below.

(a) 5 cm by 3 cm by 2 cm (b) 8 cm by 5 cm by 3 cm

(c) 10 cm by 10 cm by 10 cm (d) 4 cm by 4 cm by 4 cm

(e) 2·5 cm by 4 cm by 3 cm (f) 8·4 cm by 2·6 cm by 3·5 cm

Large volumes can be measured
in **cubic metres** (m³).

1 m³ is the volume of a cube
1 m by 1 m by 1 m.

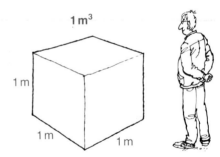

B2 Calculate the volume of cuboid 4 m by 3 m by 6·5 m.

B3 Sand for making concrete is sold in cubic metres.
Jill has ordered 5 m³ of sand from a builders' merchant.
Her friend has lent her a truck to collect it in.

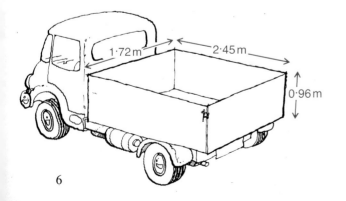

(a) How many cubic metres of sand
will the truck hold when it is
filled up level with the top?
(Give your answer to 1 d.p.)

(b) Is the truck large enough to
carry Jill's 5 m³ in one load?

B4 Calculate the volume of the 'Oxo' box shown on page 3, to the nearest cm³. (You measured the height, length and width of the box for question A4.)

B5 Box cut-out A is full-size. Calculate the volume of the box, to the nearest cm³.

B6 Box cut-out B is half full-size. Calculate the volume of the box, to the nearest cm³.

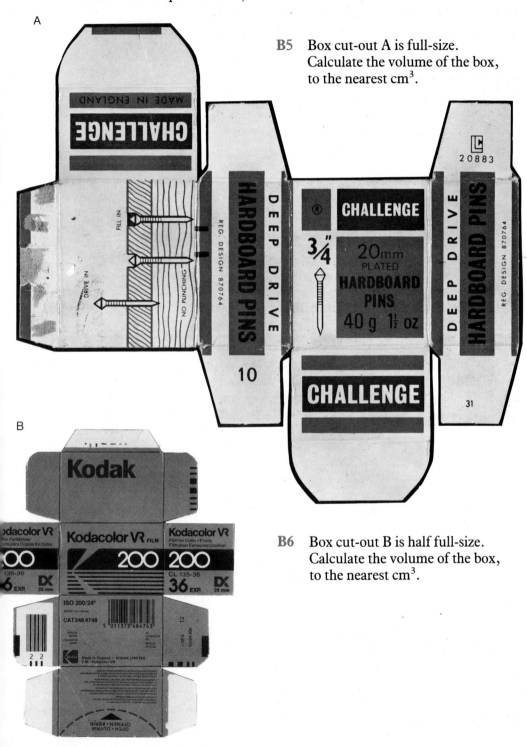

C Packing cubes

A firm makes dice, each 1 cm by 1 cm by 1 cm, and sells them in sets of 12 dice.

They want to design a cardboard box to hold 12 dice.
Someone suggests they pack the dice in 1 row of 12.

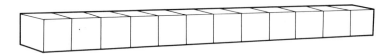

If they do that, the net of the box will look like this.
(Each square is 1 cm by 1 cm. The flaps needed for glueing are not shown.)

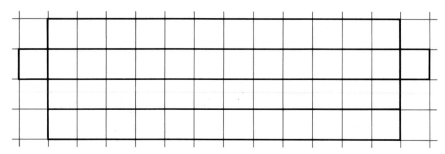

C1 What is the area of the net for this box (in cm²)?

C2 Someone suggests packing the 12 dice to make a cuboid 1 cm by 2 cm by 6 cm.

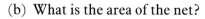

(a) Sketch (on squared paper if possible) a net for a box for this arrangement of the 12 dice.

(b) What is the area of the net?

(c) Does this box need more, or less, cardboard than the first one?

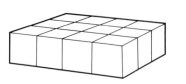

C3 Another way to pack the dice is to make a cuboid 1 cm by 4 cm by 3 cm.
Sketch a net for a box for this arrangement and find out if it uses less cardboard than the other two.

C4 The firm wants to use as little cardboard as possible.
See if there is an even better way to pack the dice than any of those suggested so far.

D Surface area

The total area of all the faces of a cuboid is called the total **surface area**.

Total surface area = Total area of all six faces = Area of net.

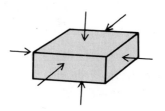
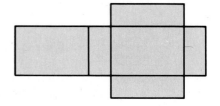

D1 Calculate the total surface area of all the six faces of this cuboid. (Do it without drawing the net.)

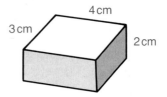

D2 Two cuboids like the one shown in question D1 are stuck together to make a single cuboid.

(a) Calculate the total surface area of the single cuboid when the two are stuck together like this.

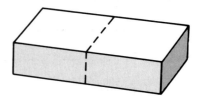

(b) Calculate the total surface area of the single cuboid when the two are stuck together like this.

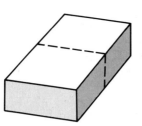

(c) Sketch another way to stick the two cuboids together to make a single cuboid.

Calculate the surface area of the single cuboid.

(d) If you wanted to make a cardboard box to hold the two cuboids, which of the three arrangements (a), (b) or (c) would need least cardboard?

D3 (a) Calculate the total surface area of a cube 1 cm by 1 cm by 1 cm.

(b) Calculate the total surface area of a cube by 2 cm by 2 cm by 2 cm. Is it 2 times as much as the surface area of a 1 cm cube? If not, how many times is it?

E Volumes of liquids

The volumes of liquids, and of containers for holding liquids, are usually measured in **litres**.

1 litre is equal to 1000 cm³.

1 cm³ is also called 1 **millilitre** (ml).

500 ml is the same as $\frac{1}{2}$ litre, or 0·5 litre.

The scale below shows how to change litres to millilitres.

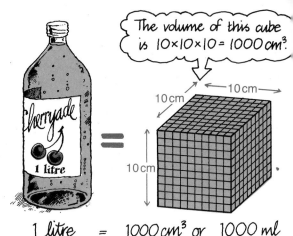

The volume of this cube is 10×10×10 = 1000 cm³.

1 litre = 1000 cm³ or 1000 ml

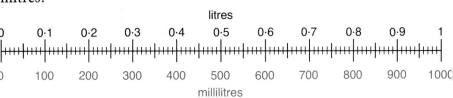

E1 Change these into millilitres.

(a) 0·6 litre   (b) 0·65 litre   (c) 0·83 litre   (d) 4·83 litres

E2 Change these into millilitres, without using the scale.

(a) 0·17 litre   (b) 0·54 litre   (c) 0·36 litre   (d) 0·361 litre

E3 Write these as decimals of a litre. Try not to use the scale.

(a) 300 ml   (b) 350 ml   (c) 940 ml   (d) 943 ml

E4 Which holds more,
these three bottles together, . . .   or these two together?

E5 (a) Calculate the volume, in cm³, of this petrol can.

(b) Write down its volume in litres, to the nearest litre.

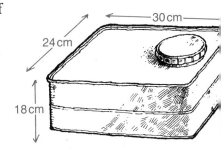

This diagram shows **1 cubic metre** split up into 1000 smaller cubes.

Each cube is the same size as the cube shown on the opposite page, and has a volume of 1 litre.

So **1 cubic metre = 1000 litres.**

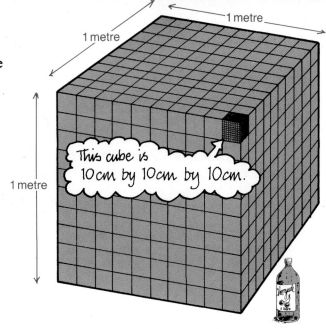

This cube is 10cm by 10cm by 10cm.

E6 A rectangular pond is 3·0 m long, 1·6 m wide and 0·5 m deep.

  (a) Calculate the volume of the pond, in m³.

  (b) Each cubic metre is equal to 1000 litres. So multiply your answer to part (a) by 1000 to find the volume in litres.

E7 A swimming pool is 24 m long and 14 m wide. The water in it is 1·6 m deep throughout.

  (a) Calculate the volume of the water, in m³.

  (b) Change the volume into litres.

  (c) How many minutes will it take to fill the pool if the water flows in at 800 litres per minute?

  (d) How many hours is this (to the nearest hour)?

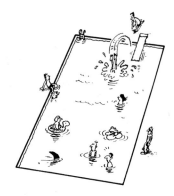

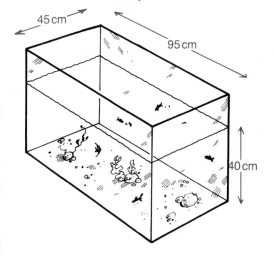

E8 How many litres of water are there in this fish tank? (Give your answer to the nearest litre.)

11

2 In your head (1)

Adding and subtracting

1 Do these in your head, as quickly as you can. Write the answers.

    (a) 8 + 6   (b) 15 + 7   (c) 28 + 3   (d) 7 + 46   (e) 35 + 9

    (f) 17 − 8   (g) 24 − 6   (h) 81 − 5   (i) 42 − 7   (j) 63 − 4

2 Do these in your head, as quickly as you can.

    (a) 29 + 30   (b) 41 + 20   (c) 63 − 30   (d) 18 + 40   (e) 67 − 20

    (f) 22 + 70   (g) 38 + 60   (h) 83 − 10   (i) 27 + 50   (j) 89 − 50

You can add a two-figure number in your head by doing it in two steps.

For example to add on 38, you can add 30 first and then 8.

So you can do 45 + 38 like this.
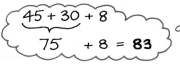

This is not the only way to add on in your head. You may have a way which you find easier. For example, some people would add on 38 by adding 40 first and then subtracting 2.

3 Do these in your head.

    (a) 26 + 33   (b) 47 + 25   (c) 34 + 57   (d) 26 + 57   (e) 18 + 34

    (f) 32 + 46   (g) 45 + 29   (h) 67 + 15   (i) 18 + 36   (j) 49 + 33

Here is a problem of the 'how many more?' type.
You are going on a journey of 63 miles. So far you have done 28 miles.
How many more miles are there?

You can do it in your head like this.   From 28 to 30 is 2 miles,
                                 from 30 to 63 is 33 miles,
                                      so **35** miles still to go.

This is not the only way to do it. Here are some others.

(1) 28 to 33 is 5   (2) 28 to 58 is 30   (3) 28 to 30 is 2
    33 to 63 is 30   58 to 63 is 5   30 to 60 is 30
        So **35**   So **35**   32 so far
                                            60 to 63 is 3
                                              So **35**

4   Work out the answer to this question in your head. Explain how you did it.

Tina is saving up for a bike. It costs £85. So far she has saved £46. How much more does she need to save?

5   In your head, work out the missing number in each of these.

(a) $44 + \mathbf{?} = 62$ (b) $28 + \mathbf{?} = 61$ (c) $14 + \mathbf{?} = 58$

(d) $33 + \mathbf{?} = 82$ (e) $58 + \mathbf{?} = 96$ (f) $\mathbf{?} + 25 = 73$

(g) $\mathbf{?} + 17 = 62$ (h) $\mathbf{?} + 44 = 80$ (i) $18 + \mathbf{?} = 72$

You can subtract a two-figure number in your head by doing it in two steps.

For example, to subtract 27 you can subtract 20 first and then 7.

So you can do $53 - 27$ like this.

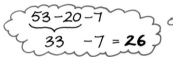

Another way to do it is to think of $53 - 27$ as the same as $27 + \mathbf{?} = 53$.

Another way is to subtract 30 first and then add on 3.

6   Do these in your head, by whatever method you find easiest.

(a) $41 - 25$ (b) $86 - 35$ (c) $73 - 59$ (d) $24 - 17$ (e) $53 - 38$

(f) $63 - 47$ (g) $95 - 37$ (h) $84 - 26$ (i) $66 - 29$ (j) $83 - 14$

7   Do these as quickly as you can in your head.

(a) A tin of beans costs 27p. How much change do you get from £1?

(b) My train leaves at 8:46. It is now 8:18. How long have I got?

(c) I picked 25 lb of apples yesterday and 39 lb today. How much altogether?

(d) I went shopping with 85p and came back with 36p. How much did I spend?

(e) It is now 4:43 and the bus goes at 5:18. How long have I got?

(f) I bought some bananas. I gave the shopkeeper £1 and got 33p change. How much did the bananas cost?

(g) How far is it from Hereford to Worcester?

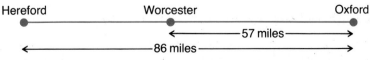

(h) I went to town by bus and train. The bus fare was 37p and the train fare 68p. How much was that altogether?

3 Graphs

A Fast and slow

In many parts of the country, especially in
hilly places, there are **springs** in the ground.
These are holes in the ground from which water
comes out.

The water is rain water which has fallen on
higher ground. It soaks into the ground until
it reaches rock which stops it soaking any
further. Then it moves along the top of this
rock until it comes to the surface as a spring.

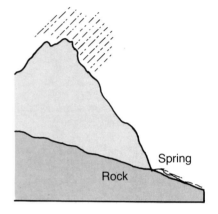

The rate of flow of a spring depends on the amount of rainfall.
In a wet season, water will come out of a spring faster than in
a dry season.

A student did a geography project about a spring near her school.
She measured the amount of water which came out in 1 minute,
2 minutes, 3 minutes, and so on.

She did this on 3rd June and on 18th September. She drew these graphs to
show her results.

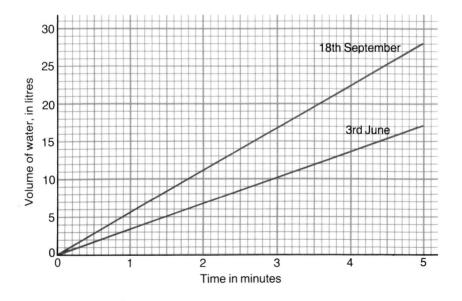

A1 (a) How much water came out in 5 minutes on 3rd June?

(b) How much came out in 5 minutes on 18th September?

(c) On which day was the spring flowing faster?

(d) How can you tell straightaway from the graph which was faster?

A2 These are the graphs for three different springs, A, B and C.

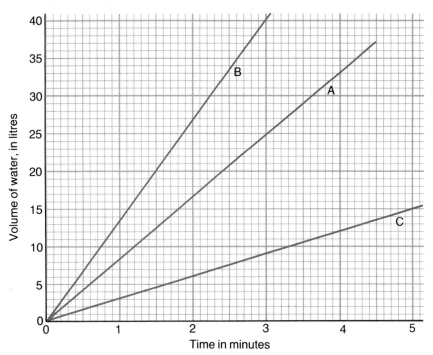

(a) Which is the fastest flowing spring?

(b) Which is the slowest flowing?

(c) How much water flows in 3 minutes from
   (i) spring A   (ii) spring B   (iii) spring C

A3 A tank is being filled from a water tap.
This graph shows the amount of water which has come out of the tap after 1 minute, 2 minutes, and so on.

Was the tap turned up (faster) or down (slower) 3 minutes from the start?

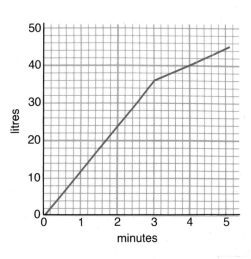

A4   This graph shows the amount of water coming out of a tap into a tank.

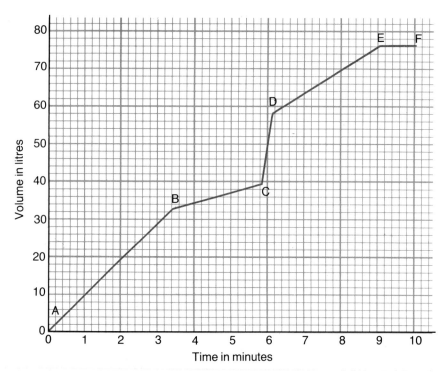

(a) What happened at B? Was the tap turned up (faster) or down (slower)?

(b) What happened at C?

(c) What happened at D?

(d) What happened at E?

(e) In which part of the graph (AB, etc.) was the tap flowing fastest?

(f) In which part was it flowing most slowly? (Do not count EF.)

You can answer all the questions in A4 without looking at the numbers on the axes of the graph.
It is the **shape** of the graph which tells you if the water is flowing slowly or fast. **The steeper the slope, the faster the rate of flow**.

A sketch graph would be enough to answer questions like those in A4.

In this sketch graph, the axes are labelled but not numbered.

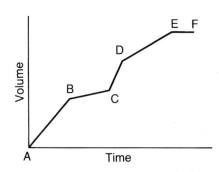

B Up and down

B1 Neeta drew this sketch graph to show what happened to the volume of water in her bath.

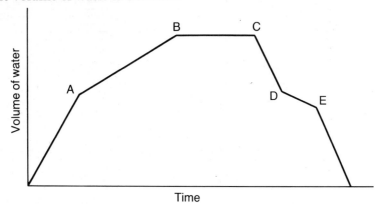

(a) Both taps were on to start with.
What could have happened at A? (There is more than one answer.)

(b) What happened at B?

(c) What happened at C?

(d) While the bath was emptying, Neeta put her foot over the plug-hole.
Which part of the graph shows this? How can you tell?

B2 Draw a sketch graph to show what happens to the volume of water in each of these 'bath stories'.

(a) Both taps were turned on together. Later both were turned off together when the bath was full. After a while, the plug was pulled out and the bath emptied.

(b) One tap was turned on to start with. Later the other tap was turned on. Both taps were turned off when the bath was full After a while, the plug was pulled out, and the bath emptied **very slowly**.

(c) Both taps were turned on until the bath was full. After a while the water was too cold so some water was emptied out. After that the hot tap was turned on until the bath was full again. Later the plug was pulled out, and the bath emptied.

(d) Both taps were turned on until the bath had filled. Then the plug was pulled out immediately. After a while the plug was replaced. Later it was pulled out again, and the bath emptied.

B3 Locks are used on canals to raise and lower boats from one level to another.

The graph below shows how the water level changes as a lock is being filled.

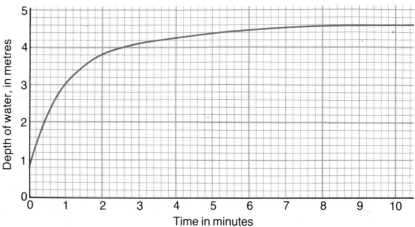

(a) In words, describe briefly what happens to the water level.

(b) What does one small square on the depth axis represent?

(c) What is the depth of the water to start with?

(d) By how much does the water rise in the first minute?

(e) By how much does it rise in the second minute (between 1 minute and 2 minutes on the time axis)?

(f) How deep is the water when the lock is full?

(g) Roughly how many minutes did the lock take to fill?

(h) When the lock empties, the water level falls quickly at first, and then more and more slowly until it has reached its lower level. Sketch a graph to show this.

B4 Here are six sketch graphs and six descriptions of tanks emptying.
Which graph goes with each description?

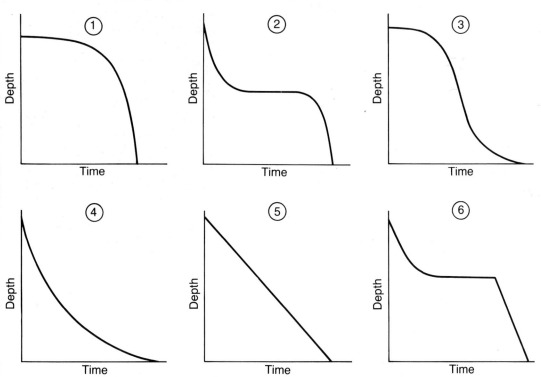

(a) The water level fell at the same speed all the time.

(b) The water level fell slowly at first, and then more and more
quickly until the tank was empty.

(c) The water level fell quickly at first, and then more and more
slowly until the tank was empty.

(d) The water level fell quickly at first and then more and more
slowly until it stopped. It stayed where it was for a while.
Then it fell quickly until the tank was empty.

(e) The water level fell quickly at first and then more and more
slowly until it stopped for a while. Then it gradually began
to fall again, falling faster and faster until the tank
was empty.

(f) The water level fell slowly at first, then quicker and quicker,
and then it fell more and more slowly until the tank was empty.

B5 Some water was heated over a burner. Its temperature rose quickly at
first, and then more and more slowly. The burner was taken away,
and the temperature fell rapidly at first, and then more and more
slowly. Draw a sketch graph to show how the temperature changes.

19

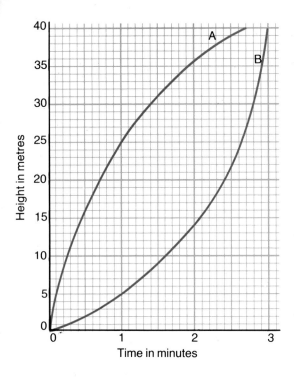

B6 Two monkeys climbed up a pole.

(a) The first one climbed up slowly at firs and then speeded up gradually. Which is this monkey's graph?

(b) In words, describe the other monkey climb.

(c) How far apart were the monkeys after (i) 1 minute
(ii) 2 minutes

(d) At what times did they pass the halfway point?

(e) One monkey stayed at the top of the pole and the other slid down, getting faster and faster. Sketch the graph for the monkey coming down.

B7 This graph shows the temperature at a place during 24 hours.

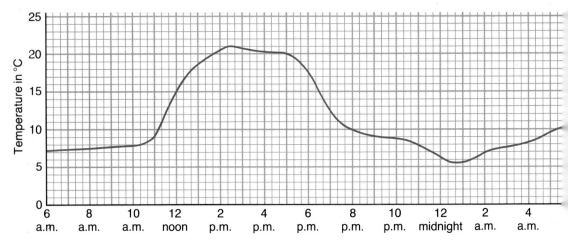

(a) What was the maximum temperature, and when did it occur?

(b) What was the minimum temperature, and when did it occur?

(c) At roughly what time was the temperature rising most quickly? Write your answer 'between . . . and . . .'.

(d) At roughly what time was the temperature falling most quickly?

(e) For how long was the temperature above 15 °C?

C Railways in Britain: growth and decline

Graphs can be used to show how the railway system in Britain has
grown and shrunk over the years.

The first railway lines were built in the early part of the 19th century.
By the end of 1832 there were 166 miles of railway open.

The table below shows how the total mileage grew between 1832 and 1851.
The map shows the railway system in 1842.

Year	Miles of railway open
1832	166
1833	208
1834	298
1835	338
1836	403
1837	540
1838	742
1839	970
1840	1479
1841	1775
1842	1939
1843	2044
1844	2236
1845	2530
1846	3136
1847	3876
1848	5129
1849	5939
1850	6559
1851	6803

C1 Draw a graph to show how the railway system grew from
1832 to 1851. Do it like this.

(a) Mark the years from 1832 to 1851 along the horizontal axis.
Space out the marks so that you can get all the years in.
You may have room to number every second year only.

```
    1832     1834     1836 . . .
```

(b) Number the vertical scale in thousands from 0 to 7000.

(c) Mark the points on your graph. You will not be able to mark the
mileage exactly. You will have to estimate where to mark each point.

(d) Join up the points. Label the axes and write a title.

The graph below shows the growth of the system from 1880 to 1930.

The map shows the system in 1914.

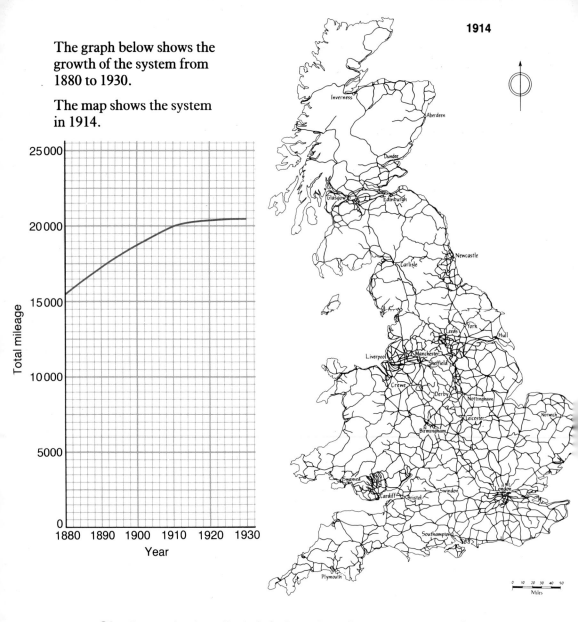

1914

Total mileage / Year

C2 In words, describe briefly how the railway system grew from 1880 to 1930.

If you look at a present-day map of the railways, you will see that there is now much less railway than in 1914. Many lines were closed in the period between 1962 and 1972. Here are the total mileages during that period.

Year	1962	1963	1964	1965	1966	1967	1968	1969	1970	1971	197
Mileage open	17500	17000	16000	14900	13700	13200	12500	12100	11800	11600	115

C3 Draw a graph to show what happened to the railways from 1962 to 1972.

22

4 In your head (2)

Multiplication and division

1 Write down the answers to these as quickly as you can.

(a) 4×3 (b) 5×4 (c) 6×3 (d) 3×9 (e) 8×5 (f) 7×7

(g) 4×8 (h) 6×6 (i) 5×7 (j) 9×4 (k) 5×5 (l) 7×4

2 Write down the answers to these as quickly as you can.

(a) 3×8 (b) 5×6 (c) 2×7 (d) 8×8 (e) 3×7 (f) 2×9

(g) 4×4 (h) 9×5 (i) 6×4 (j) 3×5 (k) 6×7 (l) 9×8

3 Write down the answers to these as quickly as you can.

(a) $20 \div 2$ (b) $40 \div 5$ (c) $16 \div 8$ (d) $18 \div 3$ (e) $24 \div 4$ (f) $30 \div 5$

$\frac{24}{3}$ ('24 over 3') means the same as $24 \div 3$.

4 Write down the answers to these as quickly as you can.

(a) $\frac{24}{3}$ (b) $\frac{15}{5}$ (c) $\frac{20}{4}$ (d) $\frac{27}{3}$ (e) $\frac{36}{9}$ (f) $\frac{50}{5}$ (g) $\frac{28}{4}$

(h) $\frac{16}{2}$ (i) $\frac{32}{8}$ (j) $\frac{45}{9}$ (k) $\frac{36}{6}$ (l) $\frac{24}{6}$ (m) $\frac{20}{10}$ (n) $\frac{64}{8}$

5 Do these as quickly as you can.

(a) 30×4 (b) 2×40 (c) 5×30 (d) 6×40 (e) 7×30 (f) 8×40

(g) 9×20 (h) 30×6 (i) 40×5 (j) 60×5 (k) 80×3 (l) 7×40

You can do 4×23 in your head like this:

Think of twenty-three as **twenty** and **three**.   4 twenties are 80. 4 threes are 12.   80 + 12 = **92**

6 Do these in your head.

(a) 5×13 (5 **tens** and 5 **threes**)   (b) 3×24 (c) 4×21

(d) 7×14 (e) 5×18 (f) 5×28 (g) 6×14 (h) 3×17

(i) 16×6 (same as 6×16)   (j) 12×8 (k) 17×7 (l) 16×4

TᴀNGʀᴀMS

You need worksheet B3–1.

The Tangram is an ancient Chinese puzzle.

You start with seven pieces, cut from a square as shown here.
You have to put the seven pieces together to make various shapes. The pieces must not overlap.

Draw a square 8 cm by 8 cm and divide it up as shown. Label the pieces and cut them out. It is better if the pieces are coloured.

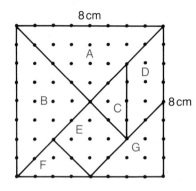

1 Use all seven pieces to make the shapes shown below and on the next page.

(Your shapes will be larger than the drawings shown here and on the worksheet.)

Use the worksheet to show how you fit the seven pieces together.
(An example is drawn on the right.)

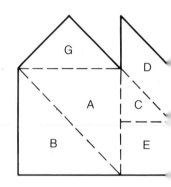

(a)

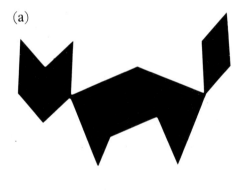

(b)

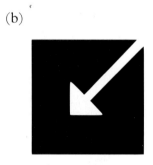

(c)

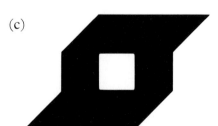

(d)

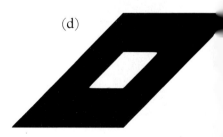

24

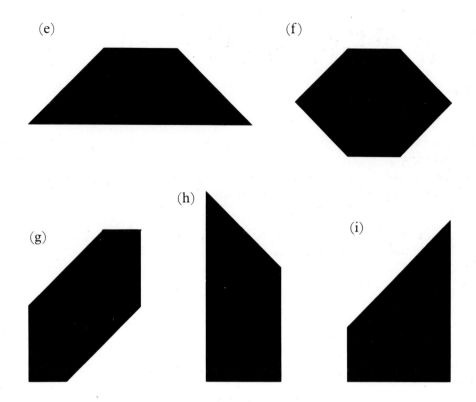

2   Draw diagrams to show how to make these shapes with all seven pieces.

(a) A rectangle   (b) A right-angled triangle   (c) A parallelogram

3   The Tangram Mystery

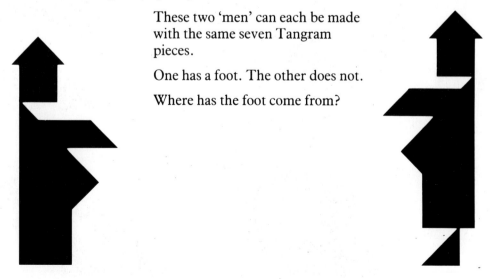

These two 'men' can each be made with the same seven Tangram pieces.

One has a foot. The other does not.

Where has the foot come from?

5 The language of algebra

A A review of some shorthand

The language of mathematics is international.
You may not know what language this problem is written in,
but the algebra is the same as you would find in an English book.

I.82. Să se arate că expresia

$$E = 4n^2 - 2n + 13$$

nu se imparte exact la 289, pentru nici un număr n intreg.

The only recognisable parts of the extract below are the letters x and y,
and the formula $y = x^2$ (unless you can read Japanese!).

yが x の関数であるとき, x の変域をこの関数の**定義域**といい,

定義域の各値に対して定まる y の値の集合をこの関数の**値域**という。

関数 $y = x^2$ で, 定義域をすべての数の集合とすれば, 値域は負

でない数全体の集合になる。

The next extract is in Arabic. At first sight only the signs – and = are
recognisable.

٦.نعود للمرة الثالثة الى منحنى الدالة

$$ص = \frac{١}{٣ س ٢ - ١}$$

But س and ص are the equivalents of x and y, ٢ and ٣ are
the numerals 2 and 3. Arabic is written from right to left,
so the formula above is

$$y = \frac{1}{3x^2 - 1}$$

It would be confusing if everybody used their own shorthand, so
people have agreed that

$3a$ means $3 \times a$ ab means $a \times b$ $\dfrac{a}{3}$ means $a \div 3$ $\dfrac{a}{b}$ means $a \div b$

A1 If a is 4, b is 2 and c is 3, work out the value of

(a) $4b$ (b) $5c$ (c) $3c$ (d) $\dfrac{a}{2}$ (e) ab

(f) bc (g) $\dfrac{a}{b}$ (h) $\dfrac{20}{a}$ (i) $\dfrac{6c}{b}$ (j) $\dfrac{ac}{b}$

A2 Electricians use the formula $V = IR$.
Calculate V when

(a) $I = 6$ and $R = 4$ (b) $I = 5$ and $R = 30$ (c) $I = 20$ and $R = 20$

A3 Another formula used by electricians is $I = \dfrac{P}{V}$.

Calculate I when

(a) $P = 16$ and $V = 2$ (b) $P = 400$ and $V = 50$ (c) $P = 56$ and $V = 7$

B Brackets

Two girls saw this sum written on the board.	One girl said it should be done like this.	The other said it should be done like this.
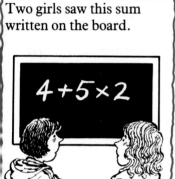	Do 4+5 first.	Do 5×2 first.

Either of the girls could be right. The person who wrote the sum on the board did not make it clear what he meant. He should have used **brackets**.

When the sum is written $(4 + 5) \times 2$, we do $4 + 5$ first.
When it is written $4 + (5 \times 2)$, we do 5×2 first.

B1 Work these out.

(a) $2 \times (5 + 3)$ (b) $(2 \times 5) + 3$ (c) $4 + (5 \times 3)$

(d) $(4 + 5) \times 3$ (e) $(12 \div 6) \times 2$ (f) $12 \div (6 \times 2)$

(g) $2 \times (3 + 2) \times 4$ (h) $(2 \times 3) + (2 \times 4)$

B2 Re-write each of these with brackets in the right places.

(a) $3 + 5 \times 4 = 23$ (b) $10 - 2 \times 3 = 4$

(c) $10 - 2 \times 3 = 24$ (d) $8 \div 2 \times 2 = 2$

(e) $40 \div 2 + 3 = 8$ (f) $40 \div 2 + 3 = 23$

B3 Do the same as in question B2 for each of these.

(a) $5 \times 4 - 2 \times 3 = 14$ (b) $5 \times 4 - 2 \times 3 = 30$

(c) $6 + 2 \times 3 + 4 = 16$ (d) $6 + 2 \times 3 + 4 = 56$

In algebra, brackets are usually left out when the spacing of the letters makes it clear what calculation to do.

For example, $pq + r$ means $(p \times q) + r$.
The p and q are close together, and that tells us to do $p \times q$ first.

If it was written $p + qr$, it would mean $p + (q \times r)$.

When you replace letters by numbers, put the brackets in.

Worked examples

(1) If p is 4, q is 3 and r is 2, work out $pq + r$.

$$
\begin{aligned}
pq &+ r \\
&= (4 \times 3) + 2 \\
&= 12 + 2 \\
&= 14
\end{aligned}
$$

(2) If a is 17 and b is 5, work out $a - 3b$.

$$
\begin{aligned}
a &- 3b \\
&= 17 - (3 \times 5) \\
&= 17 - 15 \\
&= 2
\end{aligned}
$$

(3) If u is 4, v is 3, w is 7 and x is 2, work out $uv + wx$.

$$
\begin{aligned}
uv &+ wx \\
&= (4 \times 3) + (7 \times 2) \\
&= 12 + 14 \\
&= 26
\end{aligned}
$$

B4 If a is 5, b is 4, c is 3 and d is 6, work out

(a) $ab + c$ (b) $a + bc$ (c) $b + 3d$ (d) $20 - 4c$

(e) $ab + bc$ (f) $ab + cd$ (g) $ab - cd$ (h) $ad - bc$

B5 If p is 8, q is 3, r is 4 and s is 5, work out

(a) $qr - s$ (b) $4p - 3q$ (c) $3p - qs$ (d) $pq + rs$

(e) $pr + qs$ (f) $ps - qr$ (g) $100 - 30q$ (h) $4 - 2q$

B6 If a bullet is fired vertically upwards at a speed of 160 m/s, its speed reduces gradually. If t seconds after firing its speed in m/s is s, then s and t are connected by the formula

$$s = 160 - 10t.$$

(a) Calculate the speed 12 seconds after firing.

(b) Calculate the speed 16 seconds after firing. What happens to the bullet after that?

C Rectangles

To find the area of a rectangle, you multiply the length by the width.

If the sides of a rectangle are a cm long and b cm long, the area in cm^2 is $a \times b$ or $\boldsymbol{ab}$.

Area ab

If 3 of these rectangles are put together, the total area in cm^2 is $3 \times ab$.

We write $3 \times ab$ as $3ab$.

It means $3 \times a \times b$.

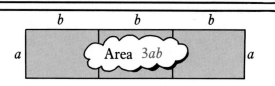
Area $3ab$

C1 (a) Work out $3ab$ when a is 2 and b is 4.

(b) Work out $4ab$ when a is 5 and b is 2.

(c) Work out $5pq$ when p is 3 and q is 2.

C2 A cuboid whose edges are a cm, b cm and c cm . . .

. . . has a net which looks like this.

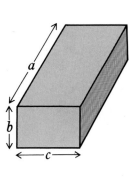

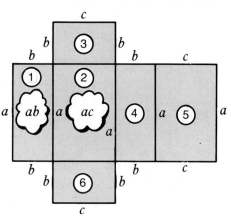

(a) The areas of rectangles 1 and 2 in the net are ab and ac. Write down the area of each of the rectangles 3, 4, 5 and 6.

(b) There are two rectangles which each have area ab. These two together have area $2ab$. There are two of area bc, and two of area ac. So the total area is $2ab + 2bc + 2ac$.

This total area is the **surface area** of the cuboid. Work out $2ab + 2bc + 2ac$ when a is 3, b is 5 and c is 4.

(c) Work out the surface area of a cuboid 2 cm by 6 cm by 3 cm.

One side of this rectangle is a cm long.

The other side is made up of two parts, one b cm and the other c cm.
So the length in cm of this side is $b + c$.

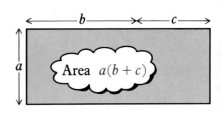

The area of the rectangle is $a \times (b + c)$.

As usual, we leave out the multiplication sign and write $a \times (b + c)$ as $a(b + c)$.

C3 (a) Work out $a(b + c)$ when a is 4, b is 2 and c is 3.

(b) Work out $a(b + c)$ when a is 5, b is 3 and c is 4.

C4 Work out $p(q + r)$ when

(a) $p = 10$, $q = 7$ and $r = 3$ (b) $p = 7$, $q = 4$ and $r = 5$

C5 If $x = 6$, $y = 4$, and $z = 1$, work out

(a) $x(y + z)$ (b) $x(y + 2)$ (c) $y(x - z)$ (d) $4(y + z)$

(e) $3(x - y)$ (f) $z(x + 2y)$ (g) $2y(x - 1)$ (h) $x(y - 4z)$

D Squaring

Just to remind you, 3^2 ('3 squared') means 3×3,
7^2 means 7×7, and so on.

| Two boys were asked to work this out. | One boy worked it out like this. He was right. | The other did it like this. He was wrong. |

We have to agree what we mean by $3 + 2^2$.

The rule which everybody agrees to stick to is this:

The squaring symbol ^{2} only squares the number or letter it is written against.

So the first boy has worked out $2 + 3^2$ correctly, and the second boy is wrong, because he squared $2 + 3$, not just 3.

D1 Work out   (a) $4 + 3^2$ (b) $10 - 2^2$ (c) 2×4^2 (d) $30 - 5^2$

D2 Work these out.

(a) $2 + 7^2$ (b) $1 + 4^2$ (c) 2×2^2 (d) $20 - (2 \times 3^2)$

(e) $2^2 + 3^2$ (f) 3×2^2 (g) $5 - 1^2$ (h) $(5 - 1)^2$

A square is a rectangle whose sides are all equal.
If the sides of a square are all a cm long, then
the area of the square in cm² is $a \times a$ or a^2.

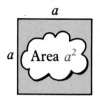

D3 Work out a^2 when a is (a) 4 (b) 3 (c) 1 (d) 5 (e) 10

D4 If a is 3, b is 5 and c is 2, work out

(a) $4 + a^2$ (b) $10 - c^2$ (c) $3 + b^2$ (d) $40 - a^2$ (e) $6 + c^2$

A cube whose edges are all a cm . . .   . . . has a net like this.
The area of every square is a^2.

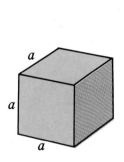

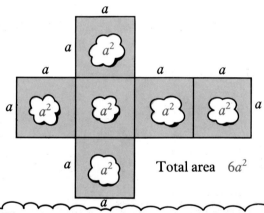

Total area $6a^2$

There are 6 squares in the net, each of area a^2.
So the total area is $6 \times a^2$, which we write $\mathbf{6a^2}$.

D5 Work out $6a^2$ when a is 3.

Check that you get the correct value for the area of the net
when a is 3. (There are 6 squares, each 3 cm by 3 cm.)

D6 Copy and complete this working
to find the value of $3a^2$ when a is 5.

$$3a^2$$
$$= 3 \times a^2$$
$$= 3 \times 5^2$$
$$=$$

31

Steve and Karen were both asked to work out $2a^2$ when a is 3.

Steve did it like this.

a is 3
so $2a$ is 6
so $2a^2$ is 6^2
$= 36$

WRONG!

Karen did it like this.

$2a^2 = 2 \times a^2$
$= 2 \times 3^2$
$= 2 \times 9$
$= 18$

RIGHT!

But why was I wrong?

$2a^2$ means 2 times a^2. You have to **square a first**, and then multiply by 2.

You did it the other way round. You multiplied by 2 and then squared.

I'll show you.

a —[square]—[×2]→

That's what Karen did.

a —[×2]—[square]→

This gives a different answer. It's wrong!

D7 If p is 3, q is 4 and r is 5, work out

(a) $2p^2$ (b) $2q^2$ (c) $3r^2$ (d) $3p^2$ (e) $2r^2$ (f) $10q^2$

D8 Suppose you drop a stone from the top of a high cliff. It will take several seconds to reach the bottom of the cliff.

It is possible to calculate where the stone is at any time during its fall. The formula for doing this is

$$s = c - 5t^2.$$

s stands for the stone's height above the bottom of the cliff, in metres.
c stands for the height of the cliff, in metres.
t stands for the time in seconds since the stone was dropped.

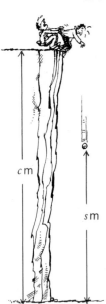

c m

s m

(a) Suppose the cliff is 80 m high. So c is 80.
Suppose the stone has been falling for 3 seconds. So t is 3.

You can calculate the stone's height, s, like this. Copy and complete the working.

$s = c - 5t^2$
$= 80 - (5 \times 3^2)$
$= \ldots$

(b) Calculate s when c is 80 and t is (i) 1   (ii) 2   (iii) 4

D9 If $q = 100 - 4p^2$, work out q when p is (a) 3 (b) 4 (c) 5 (d) 6

D10 If $y = 8x - 2x^2$, work out y when x is (a) 1 (b) 2 (c) 3 (d) 4 (e) 5

D11 A shop sells do-it-yourself double-glazing panels. The cost of a square panel with sides s feet long is given by the formula

$$c = 3s + \tfrac{1}{2}s^2$$

c stands for the cost in £.

Use the formula to find the cost of a square panel with sides

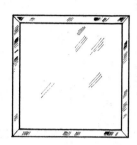

(a) 2 feet long (b) 3 feet long (c) 4 feet long

(d) 5 feet long (e) 6 feet long (f) 10 feet long

E Division

In algebra, $a \div b$ is written $\dfrac{a}{b}$.

$\dfrac{a+b}{c}$ means $(a + b)$ divided by c. So $\dfrac{12+4}{2} = \dfrac{16}{2} = 8$.

$\dfrac{a}{b+c}$ means a divided by $(b + c)$. So $\dfrac{12}{4+2} = \dfrac{12}{6} = 2$.

Worked examples

If $a = 40$, $b = 8$ and $c = 2$, calculate (a) $a + \dfrac{b}{c}$ (b) $\dfrac{a+b}{c}$ (c) $\dfrac{a}{b+c}$ (d) $\dfrac{a}{b} + \dfrac{a}{c}$

(a) $a + \dfrac{b}{c}$

$= 40 + \dfrac{8}{2}$

$= 40 + 4$

$= 44$

(b) $\dfrac{a+b}{c}$

$= \dfrac{40+8}{2}$

$= \dfrac{48}{2}$

$= 24$

(c) $\dfrac{a}{b+c}$

$= \dfrac{40}{8+2}$

$= \dfrac{40}{10}$

$= 4$

(d) $\dfrac{a}{b} + \dfrac{a}{c}$

$= \dfrac{40}{8} + \dfrac{40}{2}$

$= 5 + 20$

$= 25$

E1 If $p = 4$, $q = 6$ and $r = 2$, find the value of

(a) $\dfrac{p+q}{r}$ (b) $\dfrac{q}{r} + p$ (c) $q + \dfrac{p}{r}$ (d) $\dfrac{q}{p+r}$ (e) $\dfrac{q}{p-r}$

(f) $\dfrac{q}{r} + \dfrac{p}{r}$ (g) $\dfrac{q-p}{r}$ (h) $q - \dfrac{p}{r}$ (i) $\dfrac{3p}{r}$ (j) $\dfrac{pq}{r}$

33

E2 The size of each angle in a regular polygon can be calculated by using the formula

$$a = 180 - \frac{360}{n}.$$

n is the number of sides of the polygon.
a is the size of each angle in degrees.
Calculate a if n is (a) 3 (b) 4 (c) 5 (d) 6 (e) 8 (f) 9 (g) 20

E3 Suppose the hot tap alone can fill a bath in h minutes.
Suppose the cold tap alone can fill it in c minutes.
If t minutes is the time taken when both taps are on, then t is given by the formula

$$t = \frac{hc}{h+c}.$$

Work out t if (a) $h = 6$ and $c = 3$ (b) $h = 4$ and $c = 12$

E4 If $a = 8$, $b = 10$ and $c = 4$, work out the value of

(a) $\dfrac{bc}{a}$ (b) $\dfrac{2b}{c}$ (c) $b - \dfrac{a}{c}$ (d) $b - \dfrac{a}{2c}$ (e) $\dfrac{c^2}{a}$ (f) $\dfrac{3a}{b-c}$

F Capital letters and small letters in formulas

In algebra, a capital letter and a small letter are treated as different letters. For example, if there is an r in a formula, then it is wrong to write R instead.

Sometimes you find both in the same formula. Here is an example of a formula used by electricians.

$$I = \frac{E}{R+r}.$$

In this formula, R and r stand for different things. They are treated as different letters.

F1 Use the formula $I = \dfrac{E}{R+r}$ to work out I when

(a) E is 20, R is 2 and r is 3

(b) E is 28, R is 5 and r is 2

F2 If P is 15 and p is 7, work out the value of

(a) $\dfrac{P}{p-2}$ (b) $\dfrac{P+p}{2}$ (c) $P - 2p$ (d) $2P - 3p$ (e) $\dfrac{2P}{3+p}$

(f) $3(p-2)$ (g) $P(p-5)$ (h) $p(P-10)$ (i) $\dfrac{P-3}{p-1}$ (j) $\dfrac{p(P-}{2}$

Review 1

1 Cuboids

1.1 (a) Draw a net for the cuboid, full size.

(b) Calculate the total surface area of the cuboid.

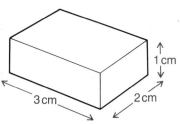

1 cm

3 cm

2 cm

1.2 Calculate the volume, to the nearest cm³, of a cuboid 6·8 cm by 4·4 cm by 10·3 cm.

1.3 The freezing compartment in a freezer is 1·45 m by 0·84 m and 0·76 m deep.

Calculate its volume to the nearest 0·1 m³.

11·5 cm

8·5 cm

9·5 cm

1.4 Would it be possible to get 1 litre of milk into the carton shown on the left? Give the reason for your answer.

1.5 (a) Which of the cartons shown below would be most suitable for holding 500 ml? (All dimensions are in cm.)

(b) Which would be most suitable for holding 750 ml?

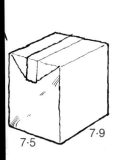

7·5

7·9

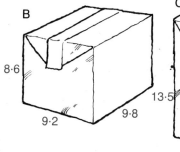

B

8·6

9·2

9·8

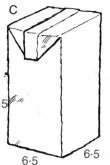

C

13·5

6·5

6·5

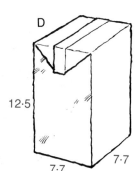

D

12·5

7·7

7·7

35

2 In your head (1)

Do these in your head as quickly as possible.

2.1 I paid 93p for a cider for Jill and a lager for myself. I know that lager costs 48p. How much does cider cost?

2.2 In a snooker match, Eric scored 84 and Bill scored 37. How many points did Eric beat Bill by?

2.3 I arrived at the dentist's at 23 minutes to four and left at 28 minutes past four. How long did I spend there?

2.4 Mita's book has 96 pages. So far she has read 38 pages. How many more has she still got to read?

2.5 Rajesh spent 48p on his lunch and 55p on a drink. How much was that altogether?

2.6 The railway from London to Portsmouth goes through Petersfield. From London to Petersfield is 55 miles. From London to Portsmouth is 74 miles. How far is it from Petersfield to Portsmouth?

2.7 A pen which used to cost 95p was reduced to 69p in a sale. How much was knocked off the price?

2.8 The tourist class air fare to Paris is £57. For an extra £15 you can travel first class. How much is the first class fare?

2.9 In a café, tea costs 17p, coffee costs 26p and cakes cost 28p each. What is the cost of

(a) tea and a cake   (b) coffee and a cake

3 Graphs

3.1 Draw a sketch graph to illustrate this 'story'.

When the Blagdon Climbers Club was started, the number of members grew slowly at first. After the TV programme about the club, the number of members grew very quickly. Then there was the accident on Perry Peak. After that, the number of members started to fall, slowly at first. The number fell faster and faster until the club went out of existence.

3.2 Three runners, David, Andrew and George, ran a race. The length of the race was 300 m.

The graphs for the three runners are shown on the next page.

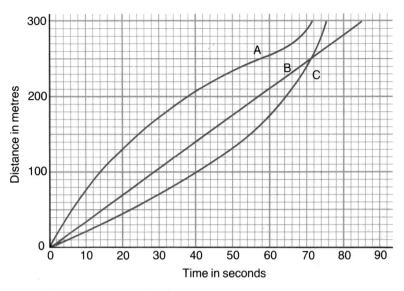

(a) David started more slowly than the others, but later on he speeded up. Which is David's graph?

(b) Andrew ran at a steady speed for the whole race. Which is Andrew's graph?

(c) Describe in words how George's speed changed during the race.

(d) In what order did the runners cross the finishing line?

(e) At what times did the runners pass the 200 m mark?

(f) During the race, one runner overtook another. Who overtook whom? When and where did it happen?

3.3 This table gives the depth of the water in a harbour during an afternoon and evening.

Time (p.m.)	2:00	2:30	3:00	3:30	4:00	4:30	5:00	5:30	6:00	6:30
Depth in m	5·2	4·6	4·3	4·2	4·3	4·5	5·0	5·6	6·2	6·8

	7:00	7:30	8:00	8:30	9:00	9:30	10:00	10:30	11:00	11:30
	7·6	8·3	8·8	9·3	9·5	9·6	9·5	9·4	9·0	8·4

(a) Draw a graph showing how the water level rose and fell.

(b) At which of these times was the water level rising fastest?

       4:00 p.m.   7:00 p.m.   9:00 p.m.

(c) What was the difference in metres between the smallest and greatest depths of the water?

37

4 · In your head (2)

4.1 Without using a calculator, write down the answers to these as quickly as you can.

(a) 4×6 (b) 5×9 (c) 2×7 (d) 6×6 (e) 8×3 (f) 10×8

(g) 5×5 (h) 4×7 (i) 9×3 (j) 4×4 (k) 6×8 (l) 3×7

4.2 Write the answers to these as quickly as you can.

(a) $15 \div 3$ (b) $28 \div 4$ (c) $40 \div 5$ (d) $36 \div 4$ (e) $20 \div 5$ (f) $18 \div 3$

(g) $35 \div 5$ (h) $64 \div 8$ (i) $50 \div 10$ (j) $18 \div 2$ (k) $32 \div 8$ (l) $30 \div 6$

4.3 Do these in your head. Write the answers.

(a) 24×3 (b) 18×4 (c) 28×3 (d) 35×3 (e) 17×5 (f) 13×4

4.4 Do these in your head.

(a) What is the cost of three 17p stamps?

(b) What is the cost of 4 tins of beans at 23p a tin?

(c) It costs 15p to go into a park. Six of us go in. How much does it cost us altogether?

5 The language of algebra

5.1 If $a = 8$, $b = 5$ and $c = 6$, calculate the value of each of these.

(a) ab (b) bc (c) $2bc$ (d) $c(a-b)$ (e) $b(a-c)$ (f) $\dfrac{c}{2}$

(g) $\dfrac{a}{4}$ (h) $\dfrac{3a}{c}$ (i) $\dfrac{a+c}{2}$ (j) $\dfrac{a}{2}+c$ (k) $a+\dfrac{c}{2}$ (l) $\dfrac{a}{2}+\dfrac{c}{3}$

5.2 If $p = 4$, $q = 10$ and $r = 3$, calculate the value of each of these.

(a) $20 - 2p$ (b) $20 - (q+r)$ (c) $\dfrac{q-p}{r}$ (d) $\dfrac{q-p}{r-1}$ (e) $4r^2$

(f) $18 - 2p^2$ (g) $2q - 3r^2$ (h) $\dfrac{q^2}{p}$ (i) $\dfrac{p^2}{2}$ (j) $5r^2$ (k) $\frac{1}{2}q^2$

5.3 If $x = 2$, $y = 4$ and $z = 5$, calculate the value of each of these.

(a) $30 - 3x^2$ (b) $50 - 2z^2$ (c) $1 + \frac{1}{2}y^2$ (d) $\dfrac{yz}{x}$ (e) $\dfrac{yz}{z-y}$

5.4 The depth of a well is given roughly by the formula $d = 5t^2$. d is the depth in metres; t is the time in seconds taken for a stone to hit the water after being dropped from the top.

Calculate d when t is   (a) 2 (b) 3 (c) 4 (d) 5 (e) 10

6 Percentage (1)

A Calculating a percentage of a quantity

This chart shows that 85% of butter is fat.

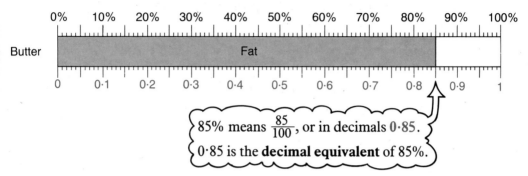

85% means $\frac{85}{100}$, or in decimals **0·85**.

0·85 is the **decimal equivalent** of 85%.

To work out 85% of an amount, you multiply the amount by 0·85.
For example, 250 g of butter . . .   . . . contains 212·5 g of fat.

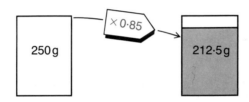

A1 Calculate the amount of fat in 450 g of butter.

A2 30% of Cheddar cheese is fat.

   (a) What is the decimal equivalent of 30%?

   (b) Calculate the amount of fat in 250 g of Cheddar cheese.

A3 20% of beef is fat.

   (a) What is the decimal equivalent of 20%?

   (b) Calculate the amount of fat in 850 g of beef.

A4 What is the decimal equivalent of

   (a) 14%   (b) 4%   (c) 9%   (d) 80%   (e) 3%

A5 What is the percentage equivalent of

   (a) 0·73   (b) 0·7   (c) 0·08   (d) 0·41   (e) 0·06

These charts are called **pie charts**.
They show the percentages of protein, fat, carbohydrate and other things
in three different baby foods.

Fruit and nut cereal

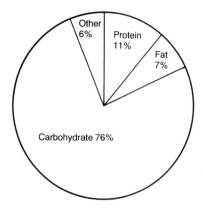

Steak and kidney casserole

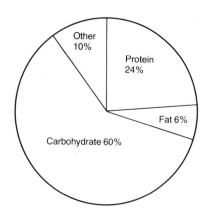

Savoury egg noodles

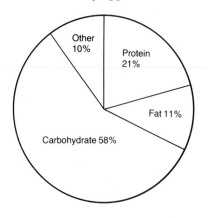

A6 Calculate the amount of protein in

   (a) 15 g of fruit and nut cereal

   (b) 15 g of steak and kidney casserole

   (c) 15 g of savoury egg noodles

A7 Calculate the amount of fat in

   (a) 35 g of fruit and nut cereal

   (b) 30 g of steak and kidney casserole

A8 Which has more protein in it,
55 g of fruit and nut cereal, or
30 g of steak and kidney casserole?

A9 During a day, a baby eats 20 g of
fruit and nut cereal, 30 g of steak
and kidney casserole and 15 g of
savoury egg noodles.

Calculate his total intake of
(a) protein
(b) fat
(c) carbohydrate

B Calculating percentages in your head

Some percentages are equal to simple fractions.

50% of something is
the same as $\frac{1}{2}$ of it.

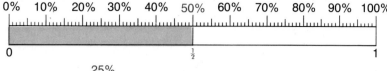

25% of something is
the same as $\frac{1}{4}$ of it.

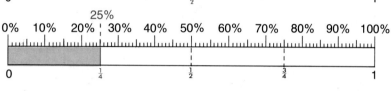

10% of something is
the same as $\frac{1}{10}$ of it.

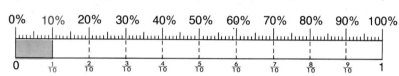

B1 Work these out in your head.

(a) 50% of £40   (b) 50% of £26   (c) 25% of 80p   (d) 25% of 32p

(e) 10% of £60   (f) 10% of 90p   (g) 10% of £240   (h) 10% of £3600

Because 10% of something is $\frac{1}{10}$ of it, you can find 10% of an amount
by dividing by 10. (But you can't find 5% by dividing by 5, or 3% by
dividing by 3!)

When you divide an amount by 10, every figure
moves one place to the right, like this.

This is how you can write down 10% of
an amount.

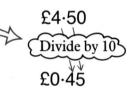

B2 Write down

(a) 10% of £3·80   (b) 10% of £12·60   (c) 10% of £13

(d) 10% of £103·80   (e) 10% of 5·80m   (f) 10% of 3·960 kg

B3 A camera shop gives a 10% discount to members of a club.
So if a club member buys a camera costing £140, the shop
takes off 10% of the price, which is £14. So the club member
pays £140 − £14 = **£126**.

What is the price to club members of these pieces of equipment?

(a) A lens costing £50   (b) A flashgun costing £45

(c) A tripod costing £18·50   (d) A filter costing £7·50

C Using your common sense

When you use a calculator to work out percentages, it is very easy to make mistakes. So you need to be able to spot silly answers.

Suppose you are calculating 62% of £86.

62% of something is more than $\frac{1}{2}$ of it, but not a lot more than $\frac{1}{2}$.

$\frac{1}{2}$ of £86 is £43. So you expect 62% of £86 to be a bit more than £43.

In fact, 62% of £86 = 0·62 × £86 = £53·32.

Each time you calculate a percentage of an amount, ask yourself:
Will the answer be a lot less than $\frac{1}{2}$ of the amount?
       or a little less than $\frac{1}{2}$ of it?
       or a little more than $\frac{1}{2}$ of it?
       or a lot more than $\frac{1}{2}$ of it?

This will help you to spot silly answers.

C1 Without using a calculator, say which of these cannot possibly be correct.

> (a) 42% of £64 = £33·20 (b) 19% of £85 = £16·15
> (c) 73% of £55 = £40·15 (d) 61% of £37 = £17·84
> (e) 26% of £92 = £23·92 (f) 83% of £124 = £67·32

C2 Use a calculator to calculate these to the nearest penny.
Think about each answer to make sure it is sensible.

(a) 38% of £60   (b) 93% of £70   (c) 14% of £36

(d) 8% of £72   (e) 73% of £160   (f) 44% of £61·50

C3 Mr Gregory, Miss Murphy and Mr Patel decide to open a restaurant. They think the restaurant will make a profit of about £1000 a month.

Mr Gregory is to be the manager. He will be paid £600 per month out of the profit. The rest of the profit is to be divided between Miss Murphy and Mr Patel. Miss Murphy will get 55% and Mr Patel will get 45%. (This is because Miss Murphy put more money into the business than Mr Patel.)

(a) In the first month, the restaurant makes a profit of £920. How much does Miss Murphy get, and how much does Mr Patel get?

(b) In the second month, the profit is £1260. How much do Miss Murphy and Mr Patel get?

D VAT

Most of the things which people pay for can be divided into **goods** and **services**.
Goods are things which you buy, such as food, furniture, clothes, records, etc.
Services are things which other people do for you, such as repairing your TV or
your motorbike.

When you pay for goods or services, you usually have to pay VAT (Value Added Tax).
This is added on to the price of the goods or services. There is no VAT on some
goods, for example food (unless you get it from a café or restaurant).

The rate of VAT is decided by the government (who get the money from the tax).
The rate changes from time to time. In 1985 it was 15%, so if the price of a
bicycle, without VAT, was £60, the VAT would be 15% of £60 = £9. So the
total cost of the bicycle would be £69.

Most shops and restaurants include VAT in their prices.

D1 (a) Find out the present rate of VAT.

(b) The cost of a ladder, not including VAT, is £28·00.
How much does the VAT come to?

(c) What is the total cost of the ladder, including VAT?

(d) What is the total cost of a shed, whose price excluding
VAT is £235?

D2 The cost of a repair at Mercury Motor Repairs is made up of

(1) labour costs, which are £14 per hour,
(2) the cost of parts, such as a new gearbox.

These two are then added together to give the total cost excluding VAT.
The customer also has to pay 15% VAT.

Complete each of these bills, to the nearest penny.

(a)

Mercury Motor Repairs	
Labour (4 hours)	£56·00
Parts	27·00
	83·00
VAT	
Total	

(b)

Mercury Motor Repairs	
Labour (11 hours)	154·00
Parts	67·50
VAT	
Total	

(c)

Mercury Motor Repairs	
Labour (6 hours)	
Parts	47·20
VAT	
Total	

(d)

Mercury Motor Repairs	
Labour (8 hours)	
Parts	29·76
VAT	
Total	

E Percentage increases and decreases

E1 Karen's rail fare for her journey to work and back is £1·35.
All fares go up by 12%.

(a) How much will be added on to her fare (to the nearest p)?

(b) What will the new fare be?

E2 If fares go up by 16%, what is the new fare if the old fare is

(a) £4·00   (b) £3·40   (c) £0·88   (d) £12·30   (e) £6·40

E3 If fares go up by 7%, what is the new fare if the old fare is

(a) £3·00   (b) £2·15   (c) £5·48   (d) £0·96   (e) £1·16

E4 Worldwings Airways decide to increase all their fares by 22%.
All new fares which are less than £100 will be rounded off to
the nearest £5.
All new fares which are more than £100 will be rounded off to
the nearest £10.

What is the new fare if the old fare is

(a) £65   (b) £130   (c) £270   (d) £420   (e) £45

E5 A clothes shop **reduces** its prices by 15% in a sale.
The normal price for a dress is £16·00.

(a) How much is taken off the price?

(b) What is the sale price of the dress?

(c) What is the sale price of a cardigan whose
normal price is £7·90? Round off the sale
price to the nearest 5p.

7 Angles and bearings

A Bearings from a point

This map shows a power station P, and the power lines leading away from it, marked *a*, *b*, *c*, *d* and *e*.

The dotted line points **north** from the power station.

You can describe the direction of each power line by giving its **bearing**. This is the angle between the north line and the power line, measured **clockwise** from north to the power line.

For example, the bearing of power line *c* is **195°**.

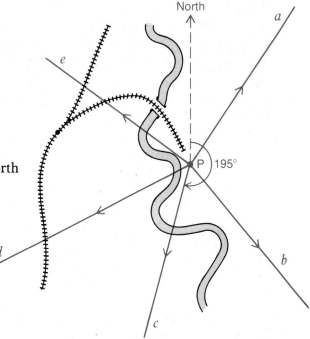

A1 Measure the bearing of each of the other power lines.

Three-figure bearings

A bearing is usually written as a three-figure number, with extra 0's written in if necessary.

So 35° becomes 035°, 7° becomes 007°, and 195° is just 195°.

A2 Measure the bearing of each direction in this diagram. Write each one as a three-figure bearing.

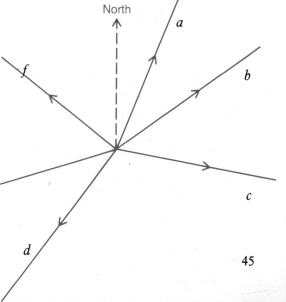

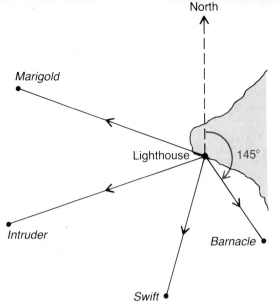

The bearing of one point from anothe[r]

This map shows a lighthouse and the positions of some ships at sea.

The bearing of the line from the lighthouse to one of the ships is called **the bearing of that ship from the lighthouse.**

For example, the bearing of the *Barnacle* from the lighthouse is **145°**.

A3 Measure the bearing of each of the other ships from the lighthouse.

A4 The scale of the map above is 1 cm to 1 km.
Measure the map and find the distance of each ship from the lighthouse.

A5 (a) Mark a point L in the centre of a page to stand for the position of a lighthouse. Draw a dotted line up the page to stand for the north line from L.

Draw a line from L on a bearing 040°.

Using a scale of 1 cm to 1 km, mark the position of a ship P whose bearing from L is 040°, and whose distance from L is 4·3 km.

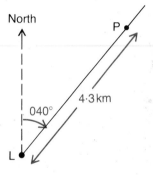

(b) On the same diagram mark the positions of the ships in the table below.

Ship	Bearing from L	Distance from L
Q	095°	3·8 km
R	152°	5·4 km
S	233°	1·2 km
T	285°	6·0 km
U	300°	3·9 km

(c) Which pair of ships is closest together? Measure the distance between them.

(d) Which pair is furthest apart? Measure the distance between them.

B Fixing a position

Various kinds of instrument can be used to measure bearings. The bearing of a ship from a place on shore can be measured by using a telescope mounted on a horizontal scale marked in degrees.

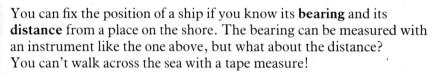

The '0' on the scale must point north.

(A simple instrument of this kind can be made from a cardboard tube.)

You can fix the position of a ship if you know its **bearing** and its **distance** from a place on the shore. The bearing can be measured with an instrument like the one above, but what about the distance? You can't walk across the sea with a tape measure!

Fortunately you do not need to know the distance. If you know the ship's bearings from **two** different points, you can fix its position.

This map shows two coast-guard stations, A and B.

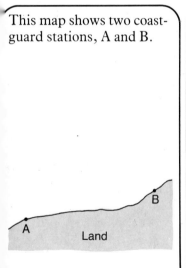

A ship in distress sends up a signal. Coastguard A measures the ship's bearing from A. It is 023°.

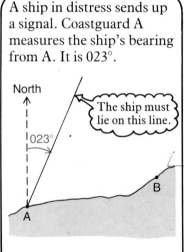

The ship must lie on this line.

Coastguard B measures the ship's bearing from B. It is 300°.

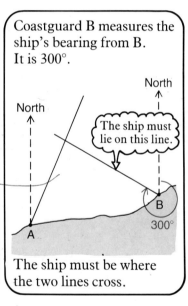

The ship must lie on this line.

The ship must be where the two lines cross.

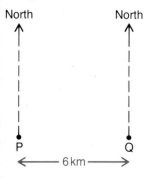

B1 In the centre of a page mark two points P and Q 6 cm apart. These stand for two coastguard stations 6 km apart. Q is due east of P.

Draw north lines at P and at Q. Use a set-square to draw the right-angles.

A ship in distress is on a bearing 049° from P and on a bearing 345° from Q. Fix its position on your diagram.

Measure the ship's distance from P and from Q.

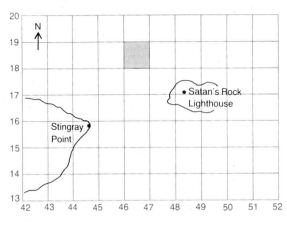

B2 *You need worksheet B3–2, which has on it a copy of this map, drawn to a larger scale.*

(a) Draw north lines at Stingray Point and at Satan's Rock Lighthouse.

(b) Copy the table below. Mark each ship's position on the map. Write in the table the four-figure grid reference of the square the ship is in. (To remind you, the coloured square's grid reference is 4618.)

Ship	Bearing from Stingray Point	Bearings from Satan's Rock	Grid reference of square
A	036°	310°	
B	108°	154°	
C	204°	232°	
D	320°	283°	
E	053°	027°	

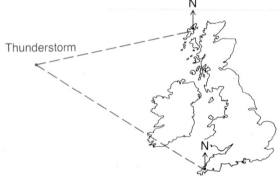

Thunderstorm

B3 *You need worksheet B3–3.*

You may have noticed crackling noises on your radio when there is a thunderstorm about. With the right equipment it is possible to 'hear' thunderstorms hundreds of miles away and to find their bearings.

If two places do this at the same time, the position of the storm can be fixed.

Two thunderstorm tracking stations are shown on the map on the worksheet. One is in Cornwall, the other on the Isle of Lewis.

These bearings were taken on a thunderstorm in the Atlantic every six hours.

Time	00:00	06:00	12:00	18:00
Bearing from Lewis	266°	262°	257°	245°
Bearing from Cornwall	294°	297°	300°	303°

(a) Mark the positions on the sheet. Write the time by each one.
(b) About what time will the storm cross the coast of Ireland?
(c) About how fast is it travelling?

c Angles of elevation

This girl is lying on the ground,
looking through a paper tube.

She is looking at a point at the
bottom of a wall. The tube is
level or **horizontal**.

She turns the tube upwards.
Now she is looking at the top of
the wall. The tube makes an angle
with the horizontal.

This angle is called the **angle of
elevation** of the top of the wall
from where the girl is lying.

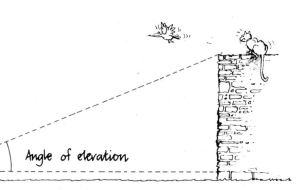

Angle of elevation

If we know the girl's distance from the wall, and we know the
angle of elevation of the top of the wall, we can make a
scale drawing and find the height of the wall.

C1 Suppose the girl is 10 metres from the wall, and the
angle of elevation of the top of the wall is 32°.

1 Let 1 cm stand for 1 metre.
Draw a horizontal line 10 cm long.
Use a set-square to draw a vertical
line at one end.

←——10 m——→

2 Draw an angle of 32° at the
other end. Now you can find
the height of the wall. Write
down the height in metres.

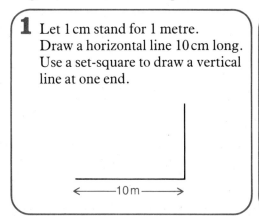

32°

?

C2 Angles of elevation are really useful when the object is
so tall that its height cannot be measured directly.

This sketch shows a very tall tree.
Make a scale drawing to find its height.

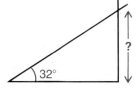

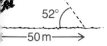

52°

←—50 m—→

C3 Make a scale drawing to find the height of this flagpole.

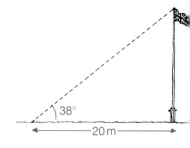

C4 Mary wants to find the height of a tree. But the tree is on the other side of a river, so she cannot measure her distance from it.

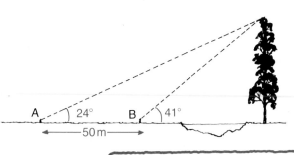

This is what she does.
First she finds the angle of elevation from where she is (A). It is 24°.

Then she walks 50 m towards the tree, to B. She measures the angle of elevation again. It is 41°.

1 Draw a horizontal line. Use 1 cm for 10 m and mark A and B 5 cm apart. (So AB is really 50 m.)

2 Draw an angle of 24° at A and an angle of 41° at B.

Where the lines cross is the top of the tree. Use a set-square to draw a vertical line from the point. Measure the height.

C5 Make a scale drawing to find the height of the wall in the sketch on the left.

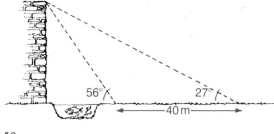

Surveyors use an instrument called a **theodolite** for measuring angles of elevation.

A theodolite is like the mounted telescope shown on page 47, but it can also be tilted upwards to measure angles of elevation.

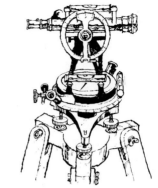

A theodolite stands on legs, so its level is above the level of the ground.

The surveyor in this picture is using a theodolite which is 1·5 m above the ground.

She has measured the angle of elevation of the top of the building.

She finds the height marked h. This is the height above the level of the theodolite. To get the total height she has to add on an extra 1·5 m.

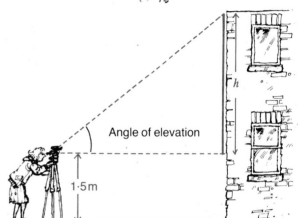

Angle of elevation

1·5 m

C6 Suppose the theodolite in the picture is 10 m away from the building. The angle of elevation of the top of the building is 37°.

Find from a scale drawing the height h.
Add on 1·5 m to get the height of the building.

C7 A surveyor places his theodolite 20 m away from a high wall. He measures the angle of elevation of the top of the wall and finds it is 61°. His theodolite is 1·35 m above ground level.

From a scale drawing find the height of the wall.

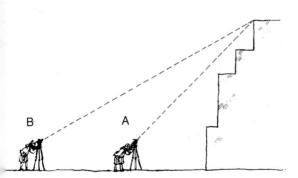

B   A

C8 The surveyor in this picture is finding the height of the building.

Her theodolite is 1·4 m above ground level.

At A the angle of elevation of the top of building is 45°.
At B it is 29°.

The distance AB is 50 m.
Find the height of the building from a scale drawing.

51

8 Percentage (2)

A Drawing pie charts

You need a pie chart scale.

44 league football matches were played one Saturday.
25 of them were home wins, 13 were away wins and 6 were draws.

We can calculate the percentage of home wins like this.

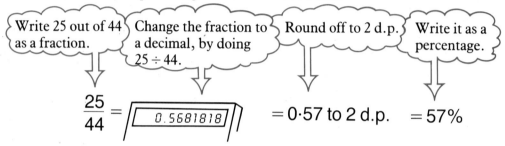

Write 25 out of 44 as a fraction. | Change the fraction to a decimal, by doing 25 ÷ 44. | Round off to 2 d.p. | Write it as a percentage.

$$\frac{25}{44} = \boxed{0.5681818} = 0\cdot57 \text{ to 2 d.p.} = 57\%$$

We can show the percentage of home wins in
a pie chart.
The 'slice' is measured with a **pie chart scale**.

Home wins

A1 (a) Calculate the percentage of
away wins.

(b) Calculate the percentage of
draws.

You will find that the three percentages add up to 101%!
This is because they were all rounded up.
When you draw the pie chart, you will have to do something about this.
You cannot get more than 100% on a pie chart.

You can either (1) Write the percentages correct to 1 d.p.

For example, $\frac{25}{44} = 0\cdot5681818\ldots = 56\cdot8\%$ (to the nearest $0\cdot1\%$)

or (2) Round **down** one of the percentages.

For example, $\frac{13}{44} = 0\cdot2954545\ldots$ Write it as 29%.

When you draw the pie chart, you cannot make each slice **exactly** the right size.

A2 Draw a pie chart to show the percentages of home wins, away wins and dr:

A3 Here are the actual results of one weekend's league matches.

Division 1					Division 2			
Arsenal	4	Luton	1		Barnsley	2	Middlesbrough	2
Aston Villa	4	Coventry	0		Burnley	1	Newcastle	0
Ipswich	2	Nottm Forest	0		Carlisle	3	Blackburn	1
Liverpool	0	Everton	0		Charlton	0	Leeds	1
Manchester Utd	1	Brighton	1		Crystal Palace	0	Chelsea	0
Notts County	2	Norwich	2		Derby	0	Sheffield Wed.	0
Southampton	4	Manchester City	1		Grimsby	1	Wolverhampton	1
Watford	0	Tottenham	1		Leicester	4	Cambridge Utd	0
West Bromwich	2	Birmingham	0		Oldham	1	Fulham	0
West Ham	1	Stoke	1		QPR	4	Rotherham	0
					Shrewsbury	1	Bolton	0

Division 3					Division 4			
Bradford City	0	Brentford	1		Aldershot	2	York City	3
Bristol Rovers	2	Southend	2		Bury	3	Chester	2
Gillingham	1	Portsmouth	0		Crewe	3	Blackpool	1
Huddersfield	0	Bournemouth	0		Hereford	2	Halifax	0
Lincoln	2	Chesterfield	0		Mansfield	1	Colchester	1
Newport	1	Reading	0		Northampton	2	Scunthorpe	1
Plymouth	1	Doncaster	2		Peterborough	1	Hull City	1
Preston	2	Cardiff	1		Port Vale	4	Rochdale	0
Sheffield Utd	3	Oxford Utd	2		Swindon	1	Darlington	2
Walsall	3	Exeter	2		Torquay	0	Bristol City	2
Wigan Ath.	0	Orient	1		Wimbledon	2	Hartlepool	0
Wrexham	4	Millwall	3					

(a) Calculate the percentages of home wins, away wins and draws.

(b) Draw a pie chart to illustrate the percentages.

B Class activity: sport on Saturday TV

B1 On the next two pages there is information about the TV programmes on one particular Saturday.

(a) Do this for each of the four channels **separately**:

    (i) Find the total broadcasting time, in **minutes**.

    (ii) Find the number of minutes given to sports programmes.

    (iii) Calculate what percentage of the total time is given to sports.

(b) Write a short report in which you compare the four channels.
Draw charts or diagrams to illustrate the percentages.

BBC 1

6.25 Open University: Reunion, by Alan Plater; **6.50** Resources for a City; **7.15** Pay for Play School; **7.40** Language Cohesion; **8.05** To Bedford, from Busso.

8.55 Heartburn: old Edgar Kennedy comedy; **9.15 The Get Set Picture Show:** New series, with Mark Curry. New and old favourites from the BBC film library.

10.45 Grandstand. The line-up is:- **10.50** Cricket (Benson and Hedges Cup Final at Lord's): Essex v Middlesex; At **1.15:** news summary; **1.20** Athletics: Preview of tonight's AAA Championship; **1.35** Racing Focus; **1.50** Ascot Racing: the 2.00; At **2.10** Cricket: back to Lord's; **2.25** The 2.35 at Ascot; **2.45** Cricket. And swimming – the Optrex ASA National Championships.

3.10 Ascot Racing: we see the King George VI and Queen Elizabeth Diamond Stakes, at 3.20; At **3.30**, more cricket from Lord's; **4.30** Swimming: back to Coventry Baths; **5.00** Final Score.

5.15 News: with Jan Leeming; **5.25** Sports round-up.

5.30 Blake's Seven: Enter Belkov (Stratford Johns), games player of great skill and small scruples (r).

6.20 Film: The Pink Panther (1964) Peter Sellers as Inspector Clouseau on the trail of an international jewel thief (David Niven). Also starring in this, the first of the many Pink Panther comedies, are Robert Wagner, Claudia Cardinale and Capucine. Director: Blake Edwards.

8.15 The Main Attraction: Variety show, with Tommy Cooper, Chas and Dave, the Kessler Twins from West Germany, the poet Pam Ayres, and Ioni and the mechanical doll. Special guest: Frankie Vaughan.

9.00 News: with Jan Leeming. And sports round-up

9.15 The Mad Death: Episode two of Sean Hignett's thriller about a rabies outbreak in Britain. Tonight, conservationists and animal owners are up in arms as the veterinary officer who is leading the fight against the outbreak (Richard Heffer) puts his tough plans into action. And yet another human victim is found. . .Co-starring Barbara Kellerman, Richard Morant and Paul Brooke.

10.05 International Athletics: The Robinsons Barley Water AAA Championships at Crystal Palace. Includes the Ready Drink Mile in which Sebastian Coe will be competing.

10.45 Kelly Monteith: The American comedian in his British-made comedy show (from BBC2).

11.15 Night Music: with the American top soul group The Stylistics. Their guest is the singer Angie Gold, dressed to match her name.

11.45 The Rockford Files: Jim Rockford (James Garner) arrives in Pastoria and runs into trouble, especially from the police.

12.45 Weather prospects for Sunday.

BBC 2

6.25 Open University (until 3.10). Begins with Computing and Road Design and ends (starts 2.45) with Modern Art: Leger.

3.10 Film: A Woman's Vengeance (1948). Drama, with Cedric Hardwicke as the doctor who sets out to prove the innocence of a man (Charles Boyer) suspected of his wife's murder. With Ann Blyth and Jessica Tandy. Directed by Zoltan Korda, from Aldous Huxley's story The Gioconda Smile.

4.45 Cricket: Live coverage of the Essex versus Middlesex match in the Benson and Hedges Cup Final at Lord's. The commentating team: Richie Benaud, Jim Laker, Tom Graveney and Ian Botham.

7.30 Gardens: Lovely pictures set to the music of Kern. Gershwin and Scott Joplin (from BBC 1).

7.45 News: and sports round-up.

8.00 Jorge Bolet Masterclass: First of three programmes featuring the great Cuban American pianist who tonight takes two young concert pianists through the first movement of the Rachmaninov Piano Concerto No 3. They are Ira Levin and Jose Feghali.

8.45 The Levin Interviews: Bernard Levin talks to the sculptor Henry Moore, now almost 85 years old, but still working seven hours a day, seven days a week. This is the last programme in Mr Levin's present series of interviews.

9.15 Murder in the First Degree: The end of the trial of Thomas Perri, accused of killing Henry Peelle in a bedroom overlooking Miami Beach. All the principal characters in the trial talk frankly about their roles in the drama (r).

10.05 Film: Dracula's Daughter (1936*). Gloria Holden plays the lady vampire with her sights on a young man (Otto Kruger), living in London. Director: Lambert Hillyer.

11.15 News.

11.20 Film: Son of Frankenstein (1939). The Monster (Karloff) has as new companion, a man who has survived the gallows (Bela Lugosi). Basil Rathbone plays the original Dr Frankenstein's scion. A vigorous and spectacular shocker with impressive sets. Directed: Rowland V. Lee. Ends at **1.35 am.**

6.25 Good Morning Britain: with Henry Kelly. Includes news bulletins at **7.00, 8.00** and **8.30; Sport at 7.10;** The Paul Gambaccini magazine at **7.15;** Discussion with a special guest at **8.07;** Aerobics at **8.32**.

8.40 Summer Run: with the disc jockey Timmy Mallett. Includes a trip to the Brighton Dolphinarium and an interview with the Young Magician of the Year, Richard Pearson.

9.25 LWT Information: What's on in the area;

9.30 Sesame Street: easy learning, with the Muppets;

10.30 No 73: The première of the programme's first "medieval" home movie – The Sands of Thyme.

12.15 World of Sport. The line-up is: **12.20** Moto Cross: British 500cc Grand Prix, from Farleigh Castle, Wiltshire; **12.40** Cycling: Tour de France. Highlights from the 17th, 19th and 21st stages in the Alps; **1.00** Swimming: Los Angeles Invitational;

1.15 News.

1.20 Moto Cross: back to Farleigh Castle; **1.40** The ITV Four: the 1.45 from Newcastle; **1.55** Powerboat Racing: Peter Stuyvesant London-Calais-London race; **2.10** Racing: the 2.15 from Newcastle; **2.25** Rallying: A tough challenge for Konrad Bartelski, the ski master turned rally driver; **2.40** Racing: the 2.45 from Newcastle; **2.55** Moto Cross: back to the British 500cc Grand Prix; **3.10** Racing: the 3.15 from Newcastle; **3.25** Moto Cross: further coverage; **3.50** News round-up; **4.00** Wrestling: from Derby; **4.55** Results.

5.05 News from ITN.

5.15 The Smurfs.

5.30 Happy Days: The Fonz is being overwhelmed by the restaurant business.

6.00 The Fall Guy: the UFO that robs a bank and abducts Jody (Heather Thomas).

7.00 Just Amazing: The organist and choirmaster who is totally deaf. Fantastic feats by fearless Frenchmen.

7.45 Ultra Quiz: The third stage of this £10,000 contest, with only 60 contestants left of the original 2,000. Tonight – across the English Channel.

8.30 Saturday Royal: Song and dance show, hosted by Lionel Blair, and featuring new acts. They include comedians and a magical escapologist. From Nottingham.

9.30 News.

9.45 Adult Movie: An Unmarried Woman (1978) Drama which provided Jill Clayburgh with an unenviable role as the wife who has to make a new life for herself and her teenage daughter when her husband says he wants a divorce. Co-starring Alan Bates. Director: Paul Mazursky.

12.00 London news headlines. Followed by: **The Tube:** Highlights from this pop music series, featuring Grace Jones, Soft Cell et al.

1.00 Close: with Michael Hordern.

2.15 As Good as New: How to repair your own clocks. And when not to attempt to do such a thing.

2.40 Those Marvellous Benchley Shorts: The comedian's son, Nathaniel, provides the commentary for this compilation of highlights from Benchley Senior's short films including The Treasurer's Report and How to Sleep (an Oscar winner)*.

4.14 Woody Woodpecker

4.35 Well Being: Three London area mothers-to-be explain why they have chosen different types of NHS medical care.

5.05 Brookside. Two repeated episodes.

6.00 Hot for Dogs: Non-stop dance programme which interprets the pop favourites of the day. Special guests: the group called Modern Romance.

6.30 News Headlines. And weather. Followed by:- **7 Days:** Moral and ethical points from the news.

7.00 Take the Stage: Theatrical improvisation contest between the "resident team" – Ian Hogg, Eleanor Bron and Robert Longeen – and three National Theatre players, Barrie Rutter, Yvonne Gidden and John Normington.

7.30 What Went Wrong? Part two of Jeremy Seabrook's three part history of the British Labour movement examines social and political conditions in Britain since the 1945 Labour election triumph.

9.00 Nana: Part four of this six-part French TV dramatization of the Zola classic. Tonight Nana (Veronique Genest) is tempted to return to the variety theatre.

10.10 The Heart of the Matter: Four-episode German TV version (this is part one) of Graham Greene's novel about a police commissioner, serving in west Africa, who is drawn into a web of corruption, diamond smuggling and blackmail. Starring Jack Hedley and Erica Rogers.

11.15 Film: Spawn of the North (1938*). Spectacular, action-filled tale of the conflict between Alaskan fishermen and Russian salmon pirates. With Henry Fonda, George Raft, Dorothy Lamour and Akim Tamiroff. Directed by Henry Hathaway. Ends at **1.15 am**.

Follow-up work

The programmes given here are for a Saturday in summer, outside the football season.

Do a similar survey for a Saturday during the football season.

9 Scale drawing

A Choosing a scale

Sadia and Tina were interested in the history of the town where they lived. They found out that an old cottage was going to be pulled down to make way for a new road.

They decided to make some drawings of the cottage and also to draw an accurate plan of it.

Here are some of Sadia's drawings of the cottage.

Sadia and Tina measured round the outside of the cottage.
Tina drew this rough plan with the measurements marked on it.

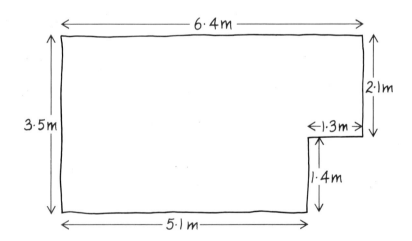

The next step was to draw a plan to scale. They decided to draw it on squared paper, because this was easier. Squared paper is useful if the angles between lines in the plan are right-angles.

Sadia suggested using a scale of 1 cm to 1 m. She started to draw the plan to this scale.

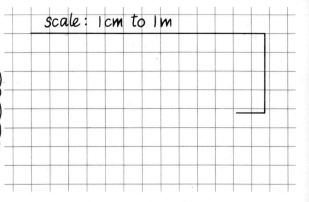

scale: 1cm to 1m

Notice that the lines of the plan do not have to be along the lines printed on the paper. But they are parallel to the printed lines.

Tina thought this plan was going to be too small. She suggested using a scale of **2 cm to 1 m**.

Sadia was not sure how long to draw each line.

The back wall of the cottage is 6·4 m long. How do I draw it on the plan?

I metre in the real cottage will be 2cm on the plan. So 6·4 m will be 6·4 × 2 cm, or **12·8 cm**.

A1 Draw a plan of the cottage on squared paper, to a scale of 2 cm to 1 m. Write the scale beside the plan.

Mark roughly the positions of the two doors of the cottage. (The pictures opposite show where they are.)

A2 If you use a scale of 5 cm to 1 m, how long would you draw each length? Start with the 6·4 m and go round the cottage clockwise. (Do not draw the plan, just say what length to make each line.)

A3 This is a sketch plan of a barn near the cottage.

(a) How long and how wide would you draw it if the scale is

    (i) 2 cm to 1 m
    (ii) 5 cm to 1 m
    (iii) 10 cm to 1 m

(b) Choose one of these scales and draw the plan to scale.

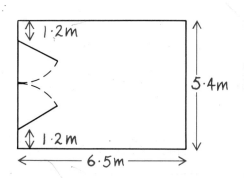

1·2m

5·4m

1·2m

6·5m

A4 This is a sketch plan of the field behind the cottage.

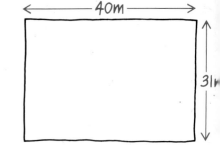

(a) How long and how wide would you draw it if your scale is 1 cm to 1 m?

(b) Would the drawing fit on a page of your book?

(c) Would it fit on your page if you used a scale of 2 cm to 1 m?

(d) Suggest a scale which you could use to draw the plan in your book. Do the drawing and write down your scale.

Useful scales

These diagrams show some scales which are useful for doing scale drawings.

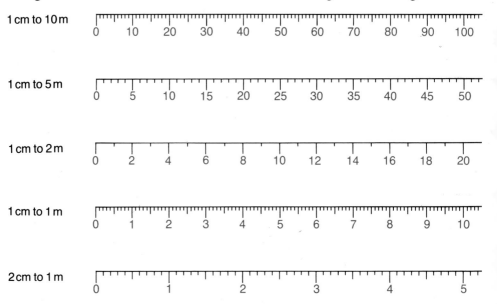

A5 Sheila's garden is 7·5 m by 4·5 m.
She wants to draw a plan of it to scale, on a sheet about the size of this page. She wants the plan to be as large as possible. Which of the scales shown above should she use?

A6 David's swimming pool is 28·3 m by 19·7 m. He wants to draw a plan of it, as large as possible, on a sheet about the size of this page. What scale should he use?

A7 A chapel is 75 m by 42 m.

(a) What scale would you use to draw a plan of it in your book?

(b) How long and how wide will the plan be, in centimetres?

B Scale calculations

Worked example

Keith is drawing a plan of a building to a scale of 1 cm to 5 m.
The building is 48 m long. How long will the plan be?

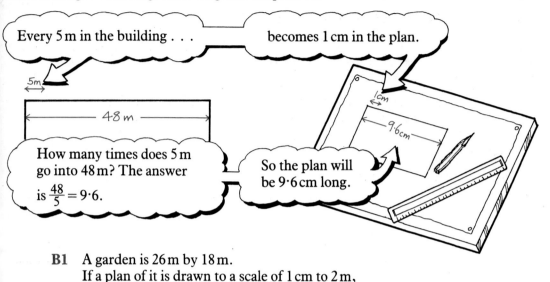

Every 5 m in the building . . . becomes 1 cm in the plan.

How many times does 5 m go into 48 m? The answer is $\frac{48}{5} = 9·6$.

So the plan will be 9·6 cm long.

B1 A garden is 26 m by 18 m.
If a plan of it is drawn to a scale of 1 cm to 2 m,

(a) how long will the plan be?

(b) how wide will it be?

B2 A rectangular car park is 132 m long and 77 m wide.
How long and how wide will a plan of it be if the scale is

(a) 1 cm to 2 m (b) 1 cm to 5 m (c) 1 cm to 10 m (d) 1 cm to 20 m

B3 **The games field problem** *You need worksheet B3–4.*

On the worksheet is a plan of a school games field. The scale
of the plan is **1 cm to 20 m**.

The groundsman has to mark out football, hockey and rugby
pitches. Their sizes, including space for goal nets and spectators, are:

Football: 120 m by 65 m   Hockey: 100 m by 55 m   Rugby: 100 m by 70 m

The school needs two hockey pitches, two rugby pitches and as many
football pitches as possible.

Each pitch can be represented by a paper rectangle, drawn
to scale and cut out. You can move the cut-outs around on
the plan of the field until you have the best arrangement.

Do this yourself, and draw your arrangement on the plan. Label
each pitch. How many football pitches did you have room for?

c What scale?

C1 These are scale drawings. The real height or length of each object is marked in red.

Measure the height or length of each drawing in cm. Write down the scale used for each drawing. It will be one of these:

1 cm to 1 m	1 cm to 2 m	1 cm to 5 m	1 cm to 10 m

2 cm to 1 m	5 cm to 1 m	10 cm to 1 m

(a)

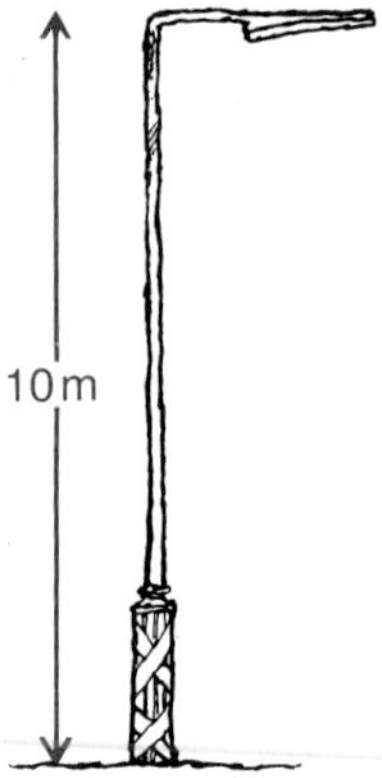

10 m

(b)

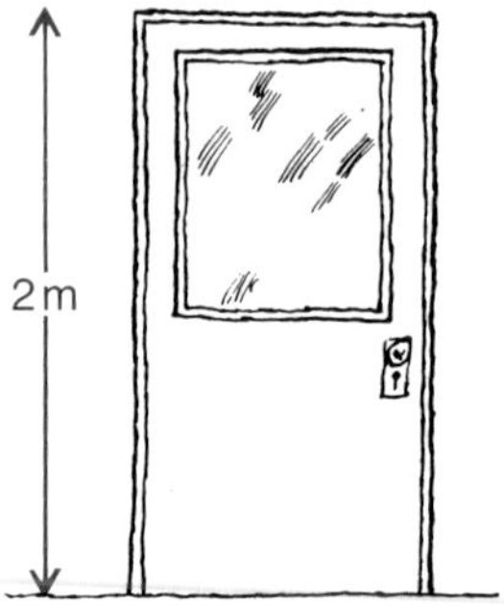

2 m

(c)

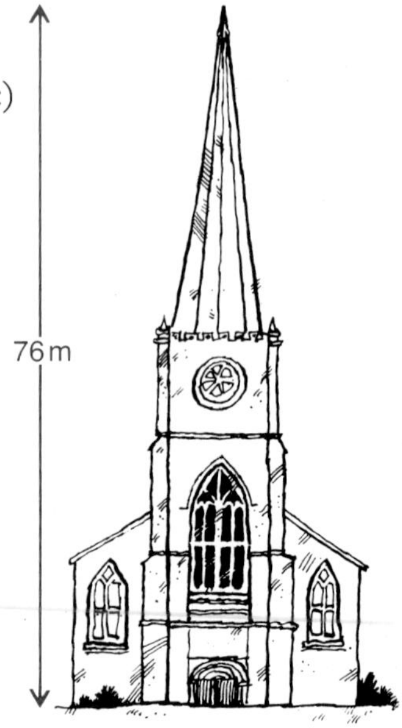

76 m

(d)

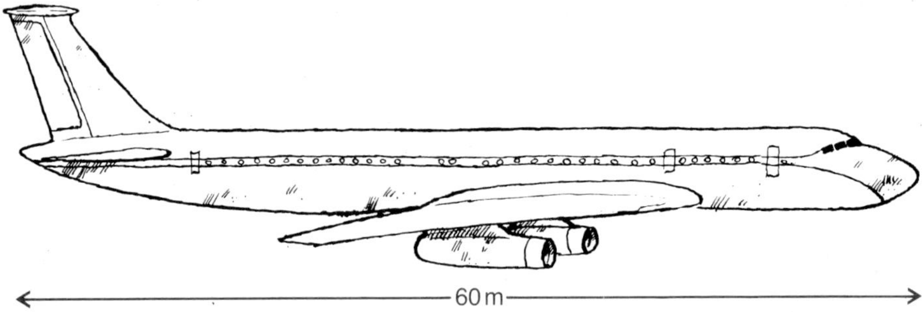

60 m

(e)

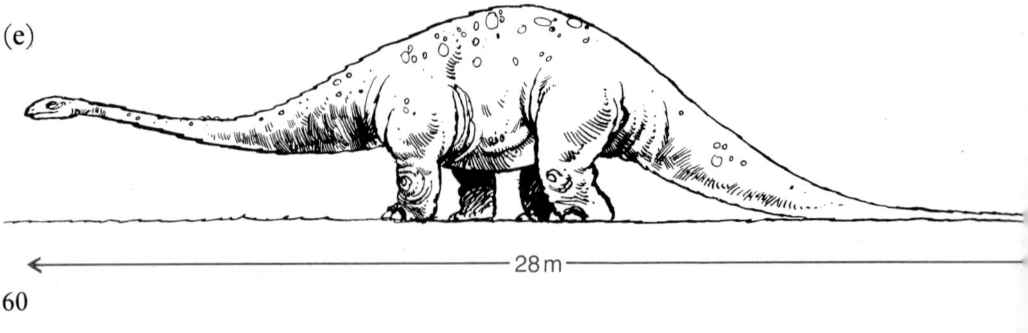

28 m

C2 These are scale drawings of familiar objects.
What do you think 1 cm stands for in each drawing?
(It will be something simple, like 2 cm, 5 cm, 50 cm, etc.)

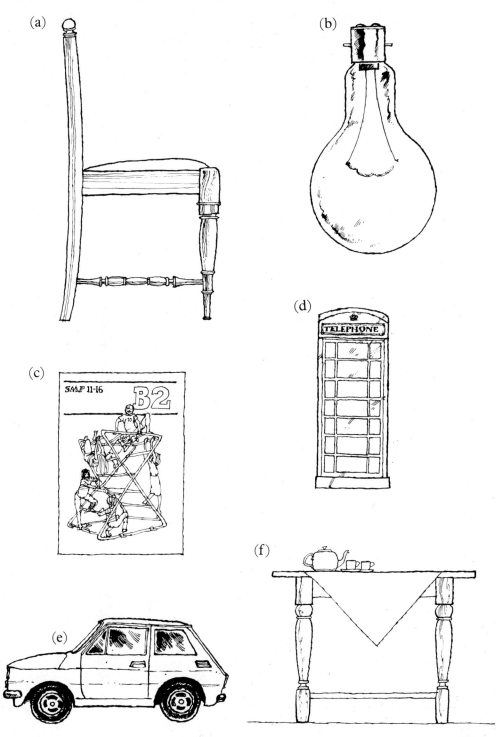

(a)

(b)

(c)

(d)

(e)

(f)

D Distances on maps

You need worksheet B3–5.

D1 Map A on the worksheet is drawn to a scale of 1 cm to 10 km. There are two radio transmitters marked on the map. One is for Radio Barset, the other for Radio Arcady. Each cross marks the position of a village.

Radio Barset's programmes can be picked up anywhere within a distance of 50 km from the transmitter.

How many villages can pick up Radio Barset's programmes? Before you do any measuring or counting, think about what would be the easiest way to see which villages are within 50 km of the transmitter. (A drawing instrument might help. Which one?)

D2 Radio Arcady's programmes can be picked up anywhere within a distance of 40 km from the transmitter.

(a) How many villages can pick up Radio Arcady?

(b) How many villages can pick up both radio stations?

D3 There are two points on the map which are exactly 50 km from the Radio Barset transmitter and exactly 40 km from the Radio Arcady transmitter. Mark them A and B on your map.

D4 Radio Arcady's transmitter is made more powerful, so that its programmes can be picked up anywhere within 60 km of it. How many villages can now pick up both radio stations?

D5 There are two points which are exactly 50 km from the Radio Barset transmitter and exactly 60 km from the Radio Arcady transmitter. Mark them C and D on your map.

D6 Map B is the map of an island, drawn to a scale of 1 cm to 1 km.

P and Q are two points on the island. The distance PQ is 9 km.

Find the point on the island which is exactly 6 km from P and exactly 5 km from Q. Label the point R. Show how you found it.

D7 Find the point in the sea which is exactly 4 km from P and exactly 6 km from Q. Label the point S. Show how you found it.

E Drawing a triangle given the lengths of its sides

E1 Draw a triangle ABC whose sides are
    AB = 7 cm   AC = 5 cm   BC = 4 cm
like this.

1 Draw the side AB first, 7 cm long.
(It is shown half-size here.)

A —————————— B

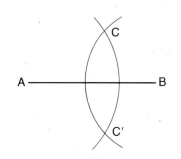

2 The point C has to be 5 cm from A
and 4 cm from B.
Find its position using compasses.
(There are two possible positions.
Mark them C and C'.)

3 The two triangles ABC and ABC'
are congruent (same shape
and size).
Draw one of them only.

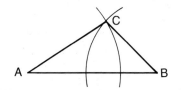

E2 Draw these triangles, full size.

(a) Triangle PQR, where PQ = 8 cm, QR = 5 cm, PR = 6 cm
(b) Triangle XYZ, where XY = 4 cm, YZ = 7 cm, XZ = 9 cm

E3 A triangular plot of land has sides of length 70 m, 58 m
and 64 m.

(a) Choose a suitable scale and draw a plan of the plot.

(b) Is it possible to build a rectangular shed 30 m by 25 m
on the plot? If you think it is possible, show where it could go.

E4 Patsy kept a pony and she wanted to draw a plan of its field.
The field had four sides. She measured the length of each
side. She called the four corners A, B, C and D.

Here are the lengths: AB = 65 m, BC = 55 m, CD = 40 m, DA = 35 m

Use a scale of 1 cm to 1 m. Can you draw a plan of Patsy's field?
If so, compare your plan with other people's.

Here are four different 'plans' of Patsy's field. Any of these plans, and a lot more, fit the measurements Patsy made.

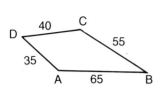 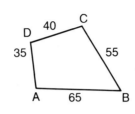 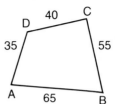 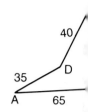

Trying to draw Patsy's field is a bit like trying to join four rods together. Their lengths are 65, 55, 40 and 35.

When they are joined together, they do not make a definite shape. The shape is 'floppy', not rigid.

You can get a rigid shape by putting in an extra rod across a diagonal. This will make the shape into two triangles, which are rigid.

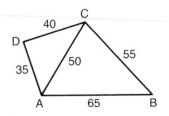

Patsy measured only the four sides of the field. This is not enough to draw the plan of the field. She should have measured across one of the diagonals as well.

So Patsy measures the diagonal AC. It is 50 m.

Here is a rough sketch of the field. It is now split into two triangles, which can be drawn accurately.

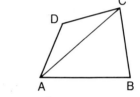

E5   Draw the plan of the field accurately, in two stages, like this.

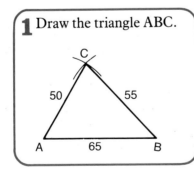 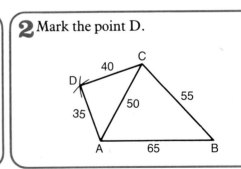

E6   Here is a sketch of another field.

(a) Draw the plan accurately to scale.

(b) Measure the distance between Q and S.

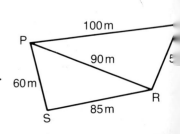

64

10 Investigation

You need triangular spotty paper.

A line 1 cm long from one dot to another will be called a **unit line**.
These are all unit lines: 　　but this is not:

There is only one kind of closed shape you can make with 3 unit lines:

There is only one kind you can make with 4 unit lines:

There is only one kind you can make with 5 unit lines:

With 6 unit lines you can make this 　　and **three** other kinds of shape.

1　Find the other three shapes you can make with 6 unit lines.
　Your shapes must be **single** shapes, not parts joined together.

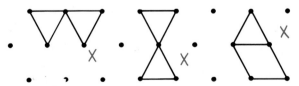

2　Find as many different shapes as you can which can be made with 7 unit lines.

3　Find as many different shapes as you can which can be made with 8 unit lines.

Review 2

6 Percentage (1)

6.1 This table shows the percentages, by weight, of protein, fat and carbohydrate in some kinds of powdered baby food.

Food	Protein	Fat	Carbohydra
English breakfast	28%	9%	58%
Savoury beef noodles	24%	4%	62%
Soft fruit yoghurt	12%	8%	75%
Chocolate and hazelnut pudding	16%	14%	65%

(a) Calculate the amount of protein in 15 g of English breakfast.

(b) Calculate the amount of carbohydrate in 30 g of chocolate and hazelnut pudding.

(c) A baby eats 20 g of savoury beef noodles and 35 g of soft fruit yoghurt Calculate his intake of (i) protein (ii) fat (iii) carbohydrate

6.2 Without using a calculator, write down

(a) 10% of £5·50 (b) 10% of £8·30 (c) 10% of 3·590 kg

(d) 50% of £84·20 (e) 25% of £5·60 (f) 10% of 12·620 kg

Heartbreak Hotel
Room prices per night

Single room without bath	£ 32·00
Single room with bath	£ 38·50
Double room without bath	£ 52·50
Double room with bath	£ 59·50

Prices do not include V.A.T.

6.3 The room prices shown on this hotel price do not include VAT.

(a) Mr Presley spends three nights in a sir room without a bath. How much does it cost without VAT?

(b) Calculate the amount of VAT which Mr Presley has to pay, at the present r

(c) Calculate Mr Presley's total bill.

Calculate the total bill, including VAT, for

(d) 5 nights in a single room with a bath

(e) 3 nights in a double room without a bath

(f) 4 nights in a double room with a bath

6.4 Heartbreak Hotel puts up its prices by 12% and rounds them off to the nearest 50p. Calculate the new price, without VAT, for each of the four types of room.

6.5 A hardware shop gives a 5% discount to members of a gardening club buying gardening tools.

What is the price to club members of these pieces of equipment? (Give the club price to the nearest penny.)

(a) A spade costing £8·45   (b) A fork costing £6·75

(c) A mower costing £74·95   (d) A trowel costing £2·49

7 Angles and bearings

7.1 Two coastguard stations A and B are 6 miles apart, and A is due north of B.

Draw a map to a scale of 1 cm to 1 mile to show the positions of A and B. (Do it in the middle of a page.)

The table below gives the bearings of a ship which is drifting out of control. Mark each position on your map, and write the time against it. Draw a dotted line to show the path of the drifting ship.

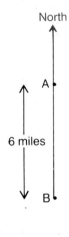

North

A

6 miles

B

Time	Bearing from A	Bearing from B
05:00	063°	032°
08:00	090°	036°
11:00	110°	045°
14:00	130°	070°
17:00	148°	099°

7.2 A surveyor was measuring the height of a tower. She used a theodolite and placed it 20 m from the bottom of the tower. The theodolite itself was 1·5 m tall.

The angle of elevation of the top of the tower was 52°. Draw a scale drawing and find the height of the tower.

8 Percentage (2)

8.1 An aircraft flew from London to Delhi via Paris. The aircraft had seats for 330 passengers.

(a) There were 228 passengers on board the flight from London to Paris. What percentage of the seats were occupied?

(b) At Paris 162 people left the aircraft and 49 joined to travel on to Delhi. What percentage of the seats were now occupied?

8.2   In a local council election, 483 people voted Conservative, 361 voted Labour and 526 voted for the Alliance.

    (a) How many people voted altogether?

    (b) What percentage of the voters voted

        (i) Conservative   (ii) Labour   (iii) Alliance

    (c) 5812 people were entitled to vote in the election. What percentage of those entitled to vote actually voted?

8.3   These tables show the numbers of votes given to each party in the general elections in 1979 and 1983 (excluding Northern Ireland). The numbers are rounded off to the nearest 10 000.

1979	
Conservative	13 700 000
Labour	11 510 000
Liberal	4 310 000
Others	1 020 000

1983	
Conservative	13 010 000
Labour	8 460 000
Liberal/SDP	7 780 000
Others	660 000

    (a) For each election calculate the percentage of the total votes given to each party.

    (b) Draw two pie charts, one for each election.

    (c) If there has been another general election since 1983, find out the figures for that election and draw a pie chart.

9 Scale drawing

9.1   This is a rough sketch of the plan of a factory.

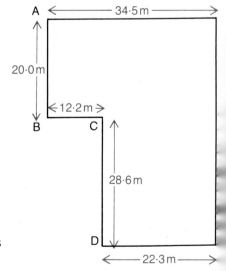

    (a) Suppose you want to draw the plan to a scale of 2 cm to 1 m. What lengths would you make AB, BC, CD, . . . and so on?

    (b) What lengths would you make AB, BC, etc. if the scale was 1 cm to 2 m?

    (c) What lengths would you make AB, BC, etc. if the scale was 1 cm to 5 m?

    (d) Choose one of these three scales and draw the plan.

9.2 These are scale drawings of well-known objects.
What do you think the scale is for each drawing? Give your reasons.

(b)

(c)

(d)

9.3 Draw a triangle whose sides are 7·5 cm, 5·5 cm and 12 cm.
Measure the angles of the triangle.

9.4 A plot of building land has four corners A, B, C and D in that
order as you go round the edge.
AB = 56 m,   BC = 39 m,   CD = 42 m,   AD = 92 m   and   AC = 78 m.

(a) Sketch a plan of the plot with the measurements on it.

(b) Draw the plan to scale. State your scale.

(c) How far is it across the plot from B to D?

M   Miscellaneous

M1   This drawing can be made into
the net of a cuboid by adding
one more rectangle to it.

(a) Draw the complete net on squared
paper. Shade the extra rectangle.

(b) If each square represents a
square 1 cm by 1 cm, calculate
the volume of the cuboid.

(c) Calculate the total surface area
of the cuboid.

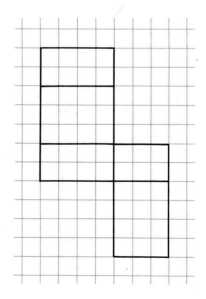

11 In your head (3)

Decimals, percentages and fractions

Answer these questions in your head, as quickly as possible.

1 (a) $4\cdot3+0\cdot5$ (b) $4\cdot7+0\cdot4$ (c) $6\cdot5+0\cdot8$ (d) $9\cdot9+0\cdot3$

2 (a) $5\cdot6-0\cdot4$ (b) $3\cdot1-0\cdot3$ (c) $4\cdot5-0\cdot7$ (d) $1\cdot3-0\cdot9$

3 What number is halfway between
   (a) 6 and 7   (b) 60 and 61   (c) $31\cdot8$ and $31\cdot9$ (d) $0\cdot5$ and $0\cdot6$
   (e) $32\cdot9$ and 33   (f) $21\cdot92$ and $21\cdot93$ (g) 51 and $51\cdot1$ (h) 0 and 0

4 Round these off to 2 decimal places.
   (a) $7\cdot0184$ (b) $24\cdot5093$ (c) $0\cdot06098$ (d) $124\cdot76495$

5 What is 10% of
   (a) £60   (b) £64   (c) £6·40   (d) £8·30   (e) £112·70

6 71 out of 180 is closest to which of these.
   20%   30%   40%   50%   60%   70%   80%

7 If 37% of the children in a school have had chicken-pox, what percentage of the children have not had it?

8 A farmer uses 28% of his land for growing wheat, 45% for growing barley, and the rest for growing oats. What percentage of his land does he use for growing oats?

9 Work these out.
   (a) $\frac{1}{3}$ of 27   (b) $\frac{1}{2}$ of 54   (c) $\frac{1}{2}$ of 92   (d) $\frac{1}{3}$ of 48
   (e) $\frac{2}{3}$ of 54   (f) $\frac{3}{4}$ of 60   (g) $\frac{3}{4}$ of 160   (h) $\frac{1}{5}$ of 75

10 Change each of these to   (i) a decimal   (ii) a percentage
   (a) $\frac{1}{2}$ (b) $\frac{1}{4}$ (c) $\frac{3}{4}$ (d) $\frac{1}{5}$ (e) $\frac{3}{5}$ (f) $\frac{7}{10}$ (g) $\frac{9}{100}$

11 Write these in order of size, smallest first.
   $1\cdot06$ $0\cdot41$ $0\cdot035$ $0\cdot57$ $0\cdot37$ $0\cdot08$ $0\cdot308$

12 Area

A Rectangles

The rectangle is the shape whose area is the easiest to calculate.

To find the area you multiply the length by the width.

For example, the area of the rectangle on the right is $5 \times 3 = 15 \, \text{cm}^2$.

If the length and width are measured in cm, the area is in cm^2.

If the length and width are in m, the area is in m^2, and so on.

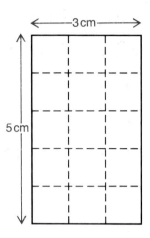

A1 Calculate the area of each of these rectangles.

(a)

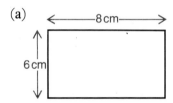

(b)

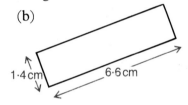

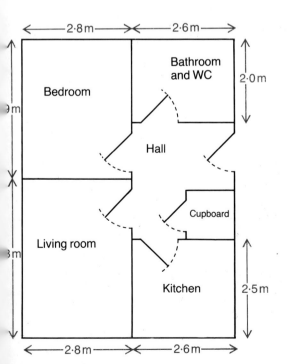

A2 This is the plan of a flat. Calculate the area of each of these rooms in m^2, to 1 d.p.

   (a) The bedroom

   (b) The living room

   (c) The kitchen

   (d) The bathroom and WC

A3 The cupboard in the flat is 1·1 m by 1·1 m.

What is its area in m^2, to 1 d.p.?

71

Some shapes can be split up into rectangles.
You can calculate the area of each rectangle
separately, and then add them together.

Usually there are different ways of splitting the
shape into rectangles.

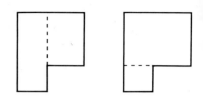

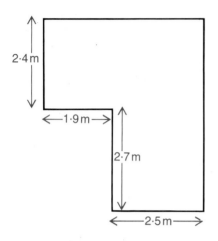

A4 The plan on the left is a plan of an
L-shaped room.

Calculate the area of the room, to the
nearest $0.1\,\mathrm{m}^2$.

A5 The diagram below is the ground plan
of a small bungalow built for an
elderly person. Calculate the area of
the bungalow, to the nearest $0.1\,\mathrm{m}^2$.

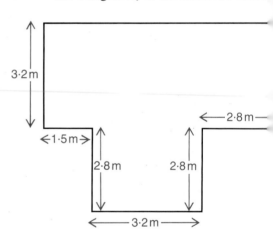

A6 Another way to find the area of an L-shape is
by subtracting.

(a) Calculate the area of the
rectangle ABCD, to the
nearest $0.1\,\mathrm{m}^2$.

(b) Calculate the area of the
grey rectangle, to the
nearest $0.1\,\mathrm{m}^2$.

(c) By subtraction, calculate
the area of the L-shape.

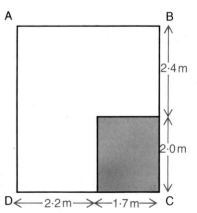

A7 Tina wants to paint the walls of her bedroom.
When the four walls of the room are 'opened out', they look
like this.

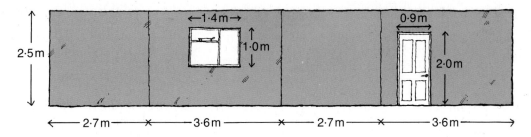

(a) Calculate the total area of wall to be painted. Set out
the steps of your calculation carefully. (Don't forget
that the areas of the door and window do not have to
be painted!) Give the area to the nearest $0.1\,m^2$.

(b) A 1-litre tin of paint will cover about $5\,m^2$. How many
tins of paint will Tina need?

(c) Does it make any difference to the answer to part (b) if
you don't bother to subtract the areas of the door and window?

A8 Sanjit has drawn up a new plan for his garden.

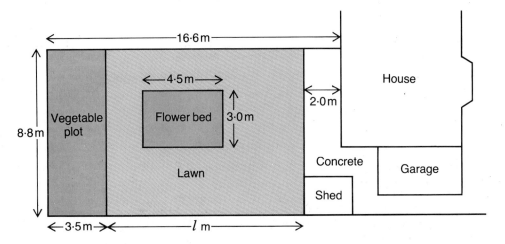

(a) How long is the lawn? (The length is marked l in the plan.)

(b) Calculate the area of the lawn (shown in red). Set out
the steps of your calculation.

(c) To make the lawn, Sanjit has to plant grass seed.
A 1 kg bag of grass seed will cover about $5\,m^2$.
How many bags will he need?

Pam has decided to paint the outside walls of her house with a special paint called 'Cemmix'.

Cemmix is sold in 10-litre drums, and the manufacturers say that 10 litres will cover about 4 m².

Pam's house is semi-detached, so it has three outside walls. They are shown in these drawings. The parts which have to be painted are shown coloured. All measurements are in metres.

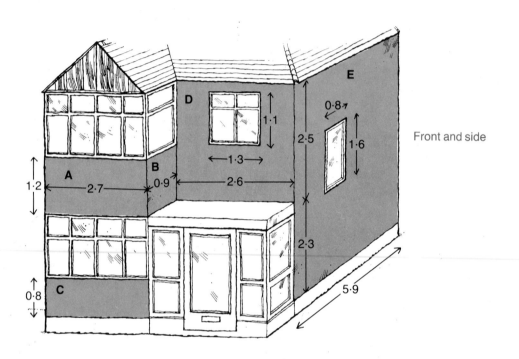

Front and side

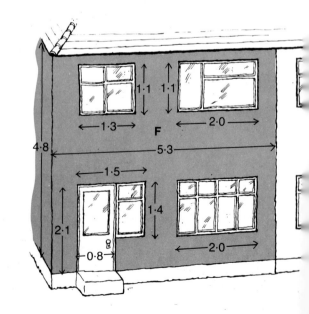

Back

(a) Calculate the areas of the coloured parts marked A, B and C.

(b) Calculate the area of the coloured part marked D.

(c) Calculate the area of the coloured part marked E.

(d) Calculate the area of the coloured part marked F.
Set out this calculation carefully, so that your method is clear.

(e) Calculate the total area of all the coloured parts.
Round off to the nearest m^2.

(f) How many 10-litre drums of Cemmix will Pam need?
(Remember a 10-litre drum will cover about 4 m^2.)

B Centimetres and metres

If measurements are given in centimetres but you want an area in
square metres, then first change the centimetres to metres.

For example, these measurements in centimetres. . .   become these in metres.

The area of this rectangle, in m^2, is $0·97 \times 1·86 = \mathbf{1·80\,m^2}$ (to 2 d.p.).

B1 Find the area of each of these rectangles in m^2, to 2 d.p.

(a) 232 cm by 48 cm   (b) 350 cm by 180 cm   (c) 69 cm by 80 cm

B2 Calculate the area in m^2 of the
cooking foil on this roll.

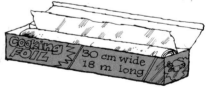

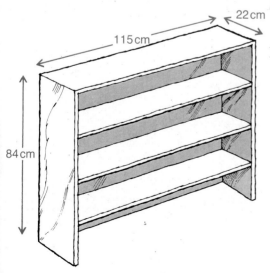

B3 Martin has made a bookcase out
of wood. Now he wants to varnish it.
He will varnish it inside and outside,
including the underneaths of the
shelves, but not the back which
stands against the wall.

(a) Calculate the total area to be
varnished in m^2, to 2 d.p.
Set out the work clearly.

(b) If one tin of varnish covers 2 m^2,
how many tins does Martin need?

C Right-angled triangles

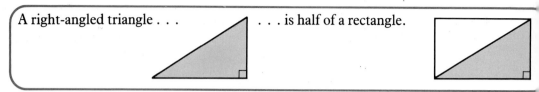

A right-angled triangle . . .   . . . is half of a rectangle.

You can find the area of a right-angled triangle . . .

4 cm

7 cm

. . . by first finding the area of the rectangle, . . .

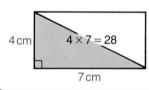

4 cm   4 × 7 = 28

7 cm

. . . and dividing it by 2.

$$\frac{28}{2} = 14\,\text{cm}^2$$

C1   Calculate the area of each of these right-angled triangles.

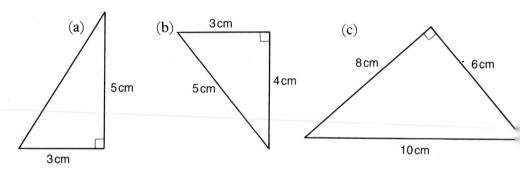

(a)

5 cm

3 cm

(b)   3 cm

5 cm   4 cm

(c)

8 cm   6 cm

10 cm

C2   Measure these right-angled triangles and calculate their areas.

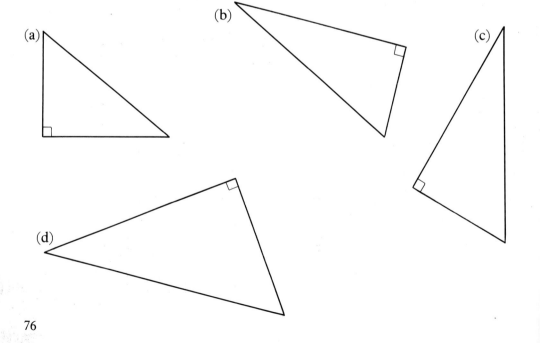

(a)

(b)

(c)

(d)

D Any triangle

1 Copy this diagram on squared paper. Colour or shade the triangle as shown.

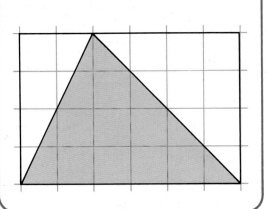

2 Cut out the rectangle. Then cut it into three pieces: the coloured triangle and two other triangles.

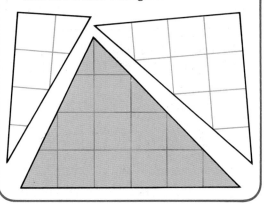

3 Put the two other triangles together. They make a triangle which is the same shape and size as the coloured triangle.

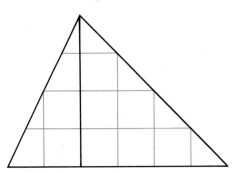

4 This shows that the area of the coloured triangle must be $\frac{1}{2}$ of the area of the rectangle.

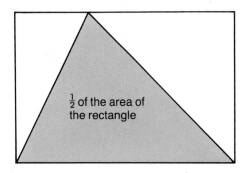

$\frac{1}{2}$ of the area of the rectangle

D1 Calculate the area of each coloured triangle.

(a)

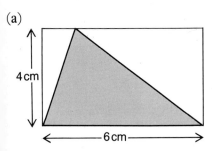

4 cm

6 cm

(b)

3 cm

10 cm

(c)

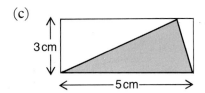

3 cm

5 cm

Suppose you want to find the area of this triangle.

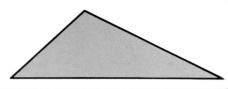

You could draw a rectangle like this. The area of the triangle will be $\frac{1}{2}$ of the area of this rectangle.

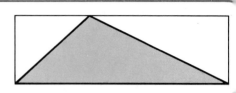

To find the area of the rectangle, you need to make these measurements.

One is the **base** of the rectangle (and of the triangle).

The other is the **height** of the rectangle (and of the triangle).

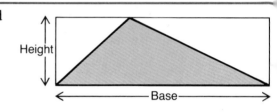

The height can also be measured here. If you do this you do not have to draw the rectangle at all. You can just imagine it.

The area of the rectangle is base × height. To find the area of the triangle you have to divide this by 2.

So the area of the triangle is $\dfrac{\text{base} \times \text{height}}{2}$

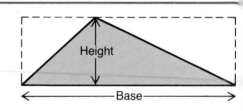

D2 Calculate the area of each coloured triangle.

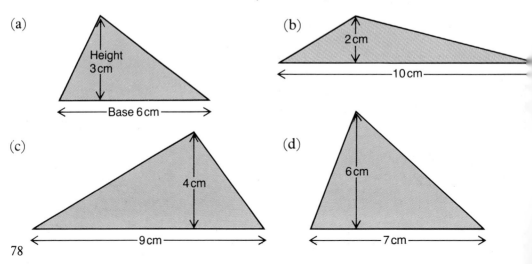

(a)   Height 3 cm   Base 6 cm

(b)   2 cm   10 cm

(c)   4 cm   9 cm

(d)   6 cm   7 cm

D3 Measure the base and height of each of these triangles.
Calculate the area of each one, to the nearest $0 \cdot 1 \, \text{cm}^2$.

Write out each answer like this: base: ...cm
height: ...cm
area: ...cm^2

Don't forget to divide by 2 when you have worked out
base × height!

(a)

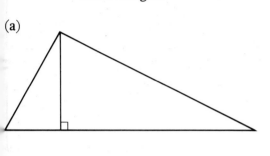

(b)

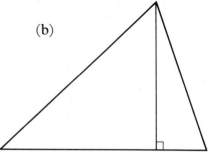

(c)

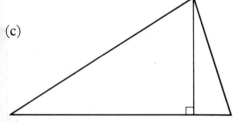

(d)

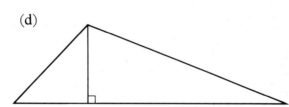

If the height of the triangle is not already drawn
you use a set-square to draw it.

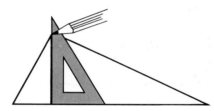

D4   *You need worksheet B3–6 (top half).*

Measure the base of each triangle on the worksheet.
Use a set-square to draw the height, and measure the height.
Calculate the area to the nearest $0 \cdot 1 \, \text{cm}^2$.

You can choose any side of a triangle to be the base.
But you must measure the height at right-angles to
the base you have chosen, using a set-square.

D5   *You need worksheet B3–6*
(bottom half).

Calculate the area of each
triangle on the worksheet.

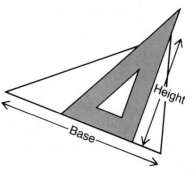

E Triangles everywhere

Any shape with straight sides can be split up
into triangles.
So if you know how to find the area of a triangle,
you can find the area of any straight-sided shape.

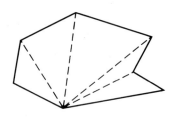

Here we will be finding the areas of some four-sided shapes,
or **quadrilaterals**.

1 A quadrilateral can be split up into
two triangles, by drawing a **diagonal**.

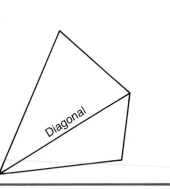

Diagonal

2 The diagonal can be used as the base
of the first triangle.
The height of this triangle must be
measured at right-angles to the base.

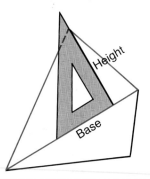

Height

Base

3 The diagonal can also be used as the base
of the second triangle.
Once again, the height must be measured
at right-angles to the base.

You can find the area of the quadrilateral
by adding the areas of the two triangles.

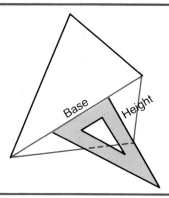

Base   Height

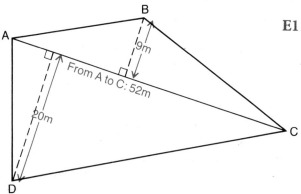

B
A
9m
From A to C: 52m
20m
C
D

E1 This is a plan of a field.

(a) Calculate the area of triangle AF

(b) Do the same for triangle ACD.

(c) Calculate the total area of
the field.

E2 This plan of a piece of building land is drawn to a scale of 1 cm to 10 m.

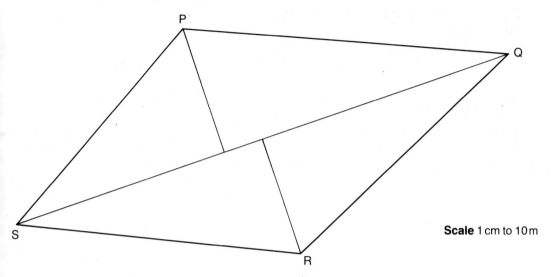

Scale 1 cm to 10 m

(a) Measure the distance SQ on the plan, in centimetres.

(b) What is the real distance SQ, in metres? (Remember that each centimetre on the plan stands for 10 metres.)

(c) Look at triangle PSQ. Take SQ as the base. Measure the height of triangle PSQ on the plan. Write down the real height in metres.

(d) Calculate the area of triangle PSQ, to the nearest m².

(e) Now calculate the area of triangle RSQ in a similar way.

(f) Add the areas of the two triangles together and write down the area of the whole piece of land.

E3 *You need worksheet B3–7.*

On the worksheet are the plans of three fields, drawn to a scale of 1 cm to 10 m.

Calculate the area of each field by drawing a diagonal to split it into two triangles. (You can draw either diagonal.) Don't forget to use a set-square to draw the height of each triangle.

E4 Jason had a chicken run. He called its four corners A, B, C and D (going round the edge) and he measured the four sides and a diagonal. His measurements were: AB = 5·3 m,   BC = 4·1 m,   CD = 3·4 m, DA = 9·6 m,   AC = 8·4 m.

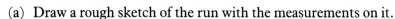

(a) Draw a rough sketch of the run with the measurements on it.
(b) Draw the plan to scale.
(c) Find the area of the run to the nearest square metre.

13 Looking at data

A Frequency charts

The word **data** means information, usually in the form of numbers.

Weather stations collect data about the weather. It consists of daily temperatures, wind speeds, and so on.

A hospital collects data about the babies born there. This data consists of weights, exact times of birth, and so on.

Here are the weights in kilograms of 50 babies born in a hospital during a period of a few days.

```
2·8  3·7  3·5  2·2  3·1  2·8  2·4  4·1  2·5  3·3
3·3  4·3  3·6  1·9  2·0  3·7  3·8  2·6  4·4  1·7
3·6  2·4  3·0  3·4  4·7  3·4  2·5  3·3  3·2  2·3
3·7  3·1  4·1  2·3  3·4  3·8  3·2  4·3  3·6  2·9
3·7  2·4  3·4  2·6  3·1  3·3  3·0  2·8  2·8  3·5
```

When you first look at this data, it is just a jumble of numbers.
But there are things you can do to get a clearer picture of the data.
It is often useful to mark the numbers on a number line.
Each spot here stands for one of the weights in the list above.

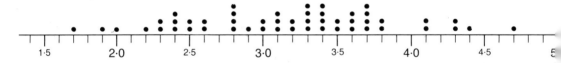

You can see at once from this diagram that there are few very heavy and very light babies, but many of medium weight.

It is often useful to **group** data.
We could group together all the weights between 1·5 and 2·0 kg,
all those between 2·0 and 2·5 kg, and so on.
We will put a weight of exactly 2·0 kg into the group **above**, 2·0 to 2·5 kg.

A1 How many babies were there in each of these groups?

(a) Between 1·5 and 2·0 kg   (Do not include 2·0.)
(b) Between 2·0 and 2·5 kg   (Include 2·0 but not 2·5.)
(c) Between 2·5 and 3·0   (Similarly.)
(d) Between 3·0 and 3·5   (e) Between 3·5 and 4·0
(f) Between 4·0 and 4·5   (g) Between 4·5 and 5·0

The number of babies in a group is
called the **frequency** for that group.

The frequencies can be shown in a
frequency chart.

The chart shows very clearly that
there are more babies of medium weight
than of very small or very large weight.

The group with the highest frequency,
3·0–3·5 kg, is called the **modal group**.

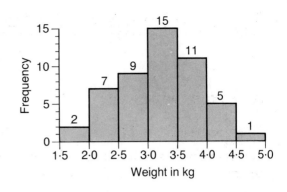

Class activity

Find out what each member of the
class weighed at birth.

Sometimes the weight is known only
in pounds (lb) and ounces (oz).
Use the conversion tables on the right
to change to kilograms.

For example,　　7 lb 5 oz

$$= 3·18\,kg + 0·14\,kg$$
$$= 3·32\,kg$$

1 lb	0·45 kg		1 oz	0·03 kg
2 lb	0·91 kg		2 oz	0·06 kg
3 lb	1·36 kg		3 oz	0·09 kg
4 lb	1·81 kg		4 oz	0·11 kg
5 lb	2·27 kg		5 oz	0·14 kg
6 lb	2·72 kg		6 oz	0·17 kg
7 lb	3·18 kg		7 oz	0·20 kg
8 lb	3·63 kg		8 oz	0·23 kg
9 lb	4·08 kg		9 oz	0·26 kg
10 lb	4·54 kg		10 oz	0·28 kg
11 lb	4·90 kg		11 oz	0·31 kg
12 lb	5·44 kg		12 oz	0·34 kg
			13 oz	0·37 kg
			14 oz	0·40 kg
			15 oz	0·43 kg

Make a tally table, like this, and find the frequency
for each group.

Draw a frequency chart. Find the modal group.
If possible, compare the chart with the one
for another class.

Weight		Frequency
1·5–2·0 kg		
2·0–2·5 kg		

and so on

A2　This is the frequency chart for a
　　group of babies.

　(a) How many babies are there in
　　　the group?

　(b) How many weighed 3·0 kg or more?

　(c) How many weighed less than
　　　4·0 kg?

　(d) What is the modal group?

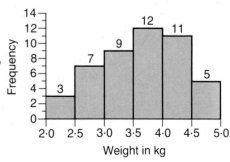

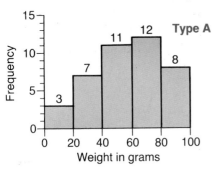

Type A

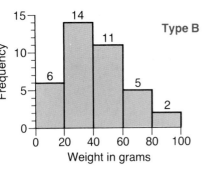

Type B

A3 A gardener grew two different kinds of tomato plant in her greenhouse. She collected all the tomatoes from each type of plant and weighed them. She drew these two frequency charts.

(a) Which of the two types of plant, A or B, produced heavier tomatoes?

(b) Write down the modal group for each type of plant.

(c) How many tomatoes did type A produce altogether?

(d) How many of them weighed less than 40 g?

(e) Calculate what percentage of the type A tomatoes weighed less than 40 g.

(f) Calculate what percentage of the type B tomatoes weighted less than 40 g.

B Mean values

The scale below shows the weights of the 8 forwards in a rugby team.

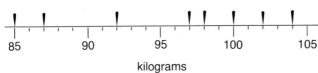

kilograms

The weights are between 85 and 104 kilograms.

It is often useful to have a single value which gives some idea of the weights (or heights, etc.) in a group.
The most common way of doing this is to calculate the **mean** of the measurements in the group.

The **mean weight** of the 8 forwards is found by adding the weights together and dividing by 8.

$$\text{Mean weight} = \frac{85 + 87 + 92 + 97 + 98 + 100 + 102 + 104}{8} = 95 \cdot 6 \text{ kg}$$
$$(\text{to 1 d.p.})$$

Here is the scale again, with the mean marked on it.
Notice that the mean is somewhere 'in the middle' of the weights.
Some of the weights are less than the mean and some are greater.

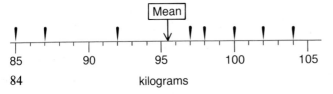

kilograms

B1 The weights of the 11 members of a football team are (in kg)

70·6, 71·5, 77·3, 77·6, 78·9, 79·3, 81·5, 82·7, 82·8, 84·1, 86·0.

Calculate the mean weight of the team.

B2 These slow-worms are drawn $\frac{1}{5}$ full-size.
Measure the length of each drawing and write down the
real length of each slow-worm.
Calculate the mean length.

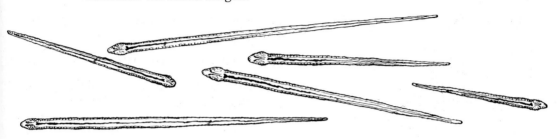

Mean values are often used to compare two sets of data.
If the mean weight of a group of boys is 51·6 kg and the mean weight
of a group of girls is 48·7 kg, we say the boys are 'on average'
heavier than the girls.

B3 Jane had seven French tests in a term. Her marks (out of 20)
were 14, 17, 12, 9, 13, 15, 13.
Neeta had eight tests. Her marks
were 11, 10, 7, 13, 16, 16, 18, 14.

(a) Calculate each girl's mean mark, to 1 d.p.

(b) Who did better on average?

*B4 These diagrams show two railway lines. In diagram (a) the red
numbers show distances between stations, in miles. In (b) they
show distances from Paddington, in miles.

For each line calculate the mean distance between stations.

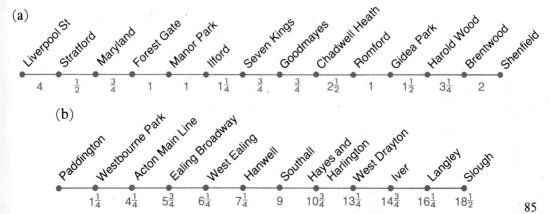

(a)

Liverpool St — Stratford — Maryland — Forest Gate — Manor Park — Ilford — Seven Kings — Goodmayes — Chadwell Heath — Romford — Gidea Park — Harold Wood — Brentwood — Shenfield

4   $\frac{1}{2}$ $\frac{3}{4}$ 1   1 $1\frac{1}{4}$ $\frac{3}{4}$ $\frac{3}{4}$ $2\frac{1}{2}$ 1 $1\frac{1}{2}$ $3\frac{1}{4}$ 2

(b)

Paddington — Westbourne Park — Acton Main Line — Ealing Broadway — West Ealing — Hanwell — Southall — Hayes and Harlington — West Drayton — Iver — Langley — Slough

$1\frac{1}{4}$ $4\frac{1}{4}$ $5\frac{3}{4}$ $6\frac{1}{4}$ $7\frac{1}{4}$ 9 $10\frac{3}{4}$ $13\frac{1}{4}$ $14\frac{3}{4}$ $16\frac{1}{4}$ $18\frac{1}{2}$

85

C Range

The two diagrams below show the weights of the tomatoes
obtained from two different tomato plants.

The mean weight is the same for each group of tomatoes.

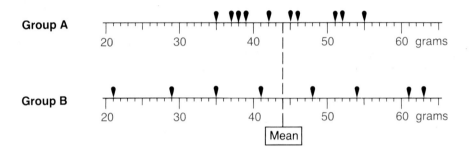

The mean weight of each group is the same, but in another way the
two groups are different from each other. The second group is much more
widely spread out than the first. The mean tells you nothing about this.

When you are describing a group of numbers (weights, heights, etc.) it is a
good idea to give the **lowest** and **highest** values as well as the mean value.

The size of the difference between the lowest and highest values is called
the **range**, and this tells you how wide the spread of the numbers is.

So the weights of the tomatoes in group A can be described like this:

Mean weight 44 g   Lightest 35 g   Heaviest 55 g   Range 20 g

C1 Describe the tomatoes in group B in the same way.

C2 Here are the weights of the boys in a seven-a-side football team, the Tigers

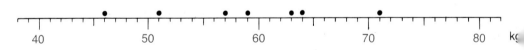

Copy and complete this 'summary' of the data:

Mean weight (to 1 d.p.)... Lightest... Heaviest... Range...

C3 (a) Do the same as in question C2 for another team, the Cheetahs,
whose weights in kilograms are   66,   49,   61,   64,   55,   65,   58.

(b) Which of the two teams is heavier on average?

(c) Which of the two is more spread out in weight?

D Limitations of the mean

A firm employing 10 people says that the
mean wage of its employees is £114 per week.

This gives the impression that £114 is a kind of 'middle' figure, with
some workers getting a bit more and some a bit less. But how much
more, and how much less? The mean tells us nothing about this.

Here are the actual wages of the 10 employees:

£40, £45, £52, £58, £65, £70, £80, £230, £240, £260.

If you add these up and divide by 10, you do get £114 as the mean wage.

Here are the wages marked on a number line.

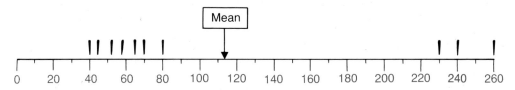

The mean gives a very misleading idea of the employees' wages.
The employees are really split into two separate groups of low and high
wage-earners.

It would be more sensible to give the mean of each separate group.

(But perhaps the firm deliberately wants to mislead people into
thinking that its workers are all quite well-paid.)

> **D1** Here are the ages of the people on a coach outing.
>
> 9, 8, 9, 9, 10, 8, 10, 10, 9, 42, 8, 9, 9, 8, 8, 53, 8, 9, 9, 10, 10
>
> (a) Does it make sense to calculate the mean age of the whole group?
> If not, why not?
> (b) Calculate the mean age of the children in the group.

> **D2** A and B are two different countries.
> In country A people earn, on average, £185 a month.
> In country B people earn, on average, £200 a month.
>
> Does it follow that people in country B are better off than
> those in country A?
>
> Give reasons for your answer. Discuss them with others in
> the class.

E Collecting data

This section consists of experiments which a whole class can do together. The first one is described in detail.

E1 Estimating a time interval of 1 minute

Each person works with a partner. You will need a watch which shows seconds. Call yourselves A and B.

To start with, A has the watch and says 'Start'.
B says 'Stop' when he or she thinks 1 minute has passed.
A notes down the number of seconds in B's 'minute'.
Then A and B change places.

(a) Draw a scale and mark the results for the whole class on it in this way.

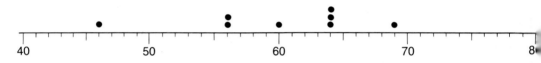

(b) Calculate the mean number of seconds in the class's estimated 'minutes'.
Mark the position of the mean on the scale.

(c) Draw a frequency chart. Use the intervals 40–45, 45–50, and so on, or smaller ones if you prefer.

Each person can mark the mean and their own estimate on the scale of the frequency chart.

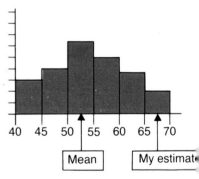

E2 Estimating the size of an angle

The teacher draws an angle on a sheet of paper and holds it up or passes it round. Each person estimates the size of the angle.

E3 Estimating the number of spots on a sheet of paper

The teacher makes some large spots on a sheet of paper (or overhead projector transparency) and shows them briefly to the whole class. Each person estimates the number of spots.

F Scatter diagrams

16 children each measured the length of their right foot and the span of their right hand. Here is the data.

footlength

handspan

Child	A	B	C	D	E	F	G	H
Foot length in cm	20	14	20	16	21	23	18	24
Handspan in cm	18	12	17	13	19	14	17	20

Child	I	J	K	L	M	N	O	P
Foot length in cm	21	19	15	23	18	25	23	19
Handspan in cm	18	14	14	18	16	22	21	15

The children wanted to know if there is any relationship between handspan and foot length.

A good way to find out is to plot the 16 pairs of values on a graph.

Each marked point stands for one of the children. It does not make any sense to try to join up the points.

This diagram is called a **scatter diagram**.

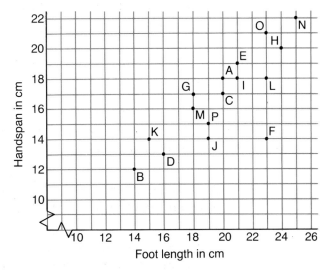

F1 Which child has long feet but quite small hands?

F2 The scatter diagram has four 'corners': top left, top right, bottom left and bottom right.

Which corner would a child go in if he or she had
(a) short feet and small hands
(b) long feet and big hands
(c) short feet and big hands
(d) long feet and small hands

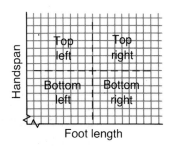

The scatter diagram above shows that the children with long feet tend to have big hands, and those with short feet tend to have small hands.

F3 **Class activity**. Draw scatter diagrams for your own class for
(a) foot length and handspan (b) height and armspan

Review 3

11 In your head (3)

Do these questions in your head as quickly as you can.

11.1 (a) $7 \cdot 7 + 0 \cdot 6$ (b) $8 \cdot 2 - 0 \cdot 8$ (c) $3 \cdot 6 + 0 \cdot 9$ (d) $2 \cdot 2 - 0 \cdot 7$

11.2 What number is halfway between

(a) $3 \cdot 3$ and $3 \cdot 4$ (b) 2 and $2 \cdot 1$ (c) $4 \cdot 9$ and $4 \cdot 91$

11.3 Write down

(a) 10% of £17·30   (b) 25% of £32·60   (c) 50% of £71

11.4 Work these out.

(a) $\frac{1}{4}$ of 72   (b) $\frac{3}{4}$ of 32   (c) $\frac{2}{5}$ of 60   (d) $\frac{2}{3}$ of 84   (e) $\frac{1}{10}$ of 84

12 Area

12.1 The measurements marked on these drawings are in cm.
Calculate the area of each coloured shape, to the nearest $0 \cdot 1 \, \text{cm}^2$.

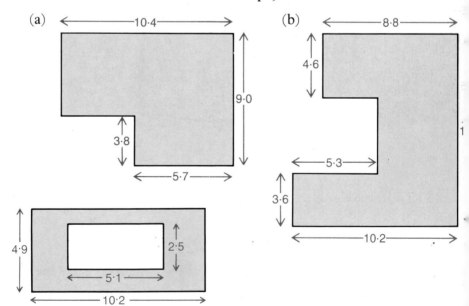

12.2 Draw accurately a triangle ABC with AB = 7 cm, BC = 9 cm and CA = 10 c
Find the area of the triangle. Show how you do it.

90

12.3 Draw this shape accurately and find its area.
Show how you do it.

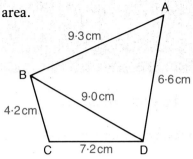

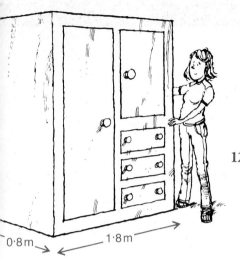

12.4 Joanne wants to varnish the front and sides of this wardrobe.

One tin of varnish will cover about $2 \cdot 5 \, \text{m}^2$.

How many tins will she need to buy?
Show how you got your answer.

13 Looking at data

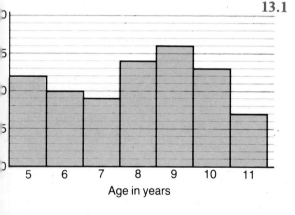

13.1 This frequency chart shows the ages of the children in a school.

(a) How many children are there in the school?

(b) What is the modal age of the children in the school?

(c) How many children are aged 8 or over?

(d) What percentage of the children are aged 8 or over?

13.2 The weights of the girls in a netball team are, in kg,

48·3, 51·7, 56·7, 53·8, 54·4, 50·2, 49·8.

The weights of the girls in a hockey team are, in kg,

49·6, 53·2, 47·7, 56·7, 51·0, 55·3, 45·4, 58·2, 57·8, 46·2, 43·7.

(a) Calculate the mean weight of the girls in the netball team, to the nearest 0·1 kg.
(b) Do the same for the girls in the hockey team.
(c) Which team is heavier on average?

M Miscellaneous

M1 A box of pins is 1 cm by 2 cm by 3 cm.

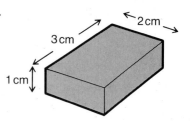

Six of these boxes are to be packed together and wrapped in transparent plastic.

Here are two possible arrangements of the six boxes.

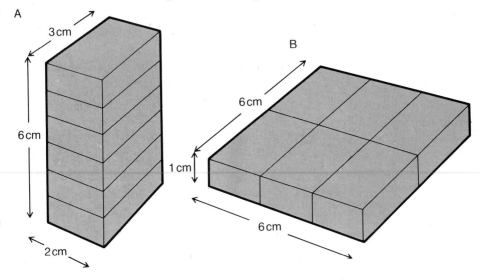

(a) Calculate the total surface area of arrangement A (the area which has to be covered with plastic).

(b) Calculate the total surface area of arrangement B.

(c) Sketch two other possible arrangements of the six boxes. (The arrangements must be cuboids.)

Call your arrangements C and D, and mark their dimensions clearly.

(d) Calculate the surface area of each of your arrangements.

(e) Which of the four arrangements A, B, your C and your D, requires the least amount of wrapping?

(f) See if you can find an arrangement which has a smaller surface area than any of those you have looked at so far.